Prince George
Fraser River
BIA
Bute Inlet
Burrard Inlet
Langley
TEXADA ISLAND
New Westminster
OUVER ISLAND
Nanaimo
Victoria
Strait of Juan-de-Fuca
Nisqually
UNITED STATES of AMERICA
Fort Vancouver April 10
Honolulu, Sandwich Is.
(Hawaii) Feb. 4
Sept. 13
Trinidad Oct. 15
Juan Fernandez I. Dec. 12
Falkland Is. Nov. 11
Cape Horn Nov. 18
GRAVESEND TO FORT VANCOUVER 1835 - 1836

S.S. BEAVER:

The ship that saved the West

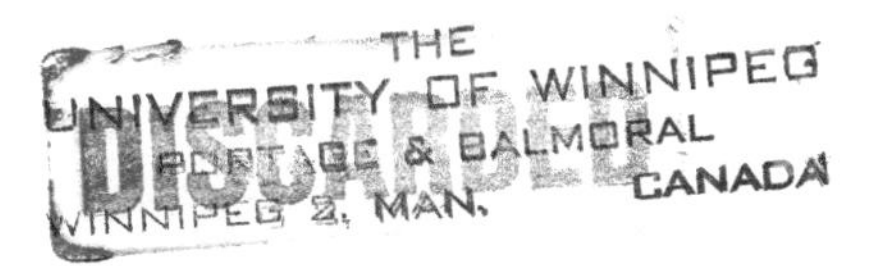

S.S. BEAVER:

The ship that saved the West

Derek Pethick

Mitchell Press Limited, Vancouver

Printed in Canada

FOR GLENN AND VELMA

BY THE SAME AUTHOR

Victoria: The Fort

James Douglas: Servant of Two Empires

"The story of the *Beaver* is the story of the early development of the west coast of Canada."

PICTURE SOURCES:

Provincial Archives, Victoria, B.C.: pages 10, 11, 30, 31, 56, 58 *(right)*, 76, 112.

Vancouver Maritime Museum, Vancouver, B.C.: pages 11 *(lower right)*, 59, 60, 61, 77, 92, 93, 94, 95, 96 *(left)*, 113 *(lower left, lower right)*, 114, 115, 116 *(top)*, 117 *(top, lower)*, 132, 133, 136.

Vancouver Public Library, Vancouver, B.C.: pages 57, 58 *(left)*, 96 *(right)*, 97, 137.

Maritime Museum of British Columbia, Victoria, B.C.: page 77.

A. C. Rogers, Burnaby, B.C.: pages 142, 143.

Mitchell Press Limited, Vancouver, B.C.: photo J. Barnard, pages 113 *(top)*, 117 *(centre, lower)*, 134, 135 *(left)*; photo R. Parkes, pages 116 *(centre, lower)*, 135 *(right)*.

Contents

Foreword

To devote an entire book to the story of a single small ship may seem, I realize, disproportionate. It can, I think, only be justified if it can be shown that the ship in question had an influence on the course of events out of all proportion to its size. This is, in fact, the claim I make for the *Beaver,* and the purpose of the pages that follow is to provide the supporting evidence. The *Beaver* was, I believe, the most important ship in the history of Canada's west coast, and if this claim can be established, the space devoted to it will not perhaps seem too great.

It will be noted that I have consistently referred to the *Beaver* as "it" instead of the more customary "she." This break with tradition seems, however, justified. The *Beaver* had many virtues, but charm was not one of them, and it had neither ancestors nor descendants. I feel, therefore, that my usage is the most appropriate one, and not even the consideration, advanced at the last minute by an anguished supporter of the older mode of reference, that when it first appeared on this coast its decks were flush, and superstructures were added later, melts my hard heart in this matter.

In assembling the material for this book, I have been conscious that the accounts on which it is based may be of varying degrees of accuracy. Those who have read and compared the four gospels will be aware that the recollections of old-timers are not always to be trusted, and similar considerations no doubt apply in the case of the *Beaver.* I have tried, however, to sift fact from fancy, and many well-known stories, as well as some interesting new ones that I have come across, find for this reason no place in the pages that follow.

My thanks are due to the Governor and Committee of the Hudson's Bay Company for permitting the use of copyrighted material, and also to the Company's Archivist for courteously answering my many questions. Also to the staff of the B.C. Provincial Archives, Victoria; Col. J. W. D. Symons of the B.C. Maritime Museum, Victoria; Daniel T. Gallacher of the B.C. Provincial Museum, Victoria; the staff of the Vancouver City Archives; Leonard G. McCann of the Vancouver Maritime Museum; Ron D'Altroy of the Vancouver Public Library; A. C. Rogers of Burnaby, B.C.; John Houghton of Mitchell Press for his invaluable assistance in assembling the illustrations and designing the book; as well as the numerous private citizens who responded to my enquiries.

DEREK PETHICK

The man on the bridge

Across the waters of Burrard Inlet, where once, long ago, Captain George Vancouver's ships cast anchor, the great bridge has been flung; in a ceaseless stream, those bound on business or pleasure pour along it. The twentieth century is rushing toward its close, speed and convenience are its watchwords, and the slightest delay can rouse the tempers of impatient motorists. Certainly, as high above the inlet they cross and recross swiftly between earth and earth, they have little time for philosophizing about the scene of which they form a part.

A few, however, on occasion make their way across the bridge on foot, and as the dusk deepens one evening, one such solitary figure may be seen to pause in his slow journey as he nears the southern shore and to look down into the tide-stirred depths below. Nothing seems to break the surface of the inlet, yet apparently the traveller finds much to hold his interest, for though the night air grows chill, he lingers as if loath to leave.

What, one wonders, does he see in these featureless grey waters?

The mystery can only be solved if we know that he is looking not with his eyes but his imagination. For what he is picturing and reflecting upon is the spot, some twenty fathoms below the surface, where a part, and by no means an insignificant part, of British Columbia history has for eighty years been resting.

Somewhere down there, in the mud and the darkness, its once sturdy timbers eaten away and only parts of its metal frame remaining, lies the hulk of the old S.S. *Beaver*. Not to many now, perhaps, a name to be conjured with; yet for much of the last century the best-known vessel on this coast. Proudly had it come to these waters in 1836, announcing a quickening of the region's economic pulse, the arrival of the age of steam; valiantly had it served its owners and the public for half a century, as it shuttled back and forth among these harbors and inlets, weaving together the fabric of a nation's life; finally, its task done, quietly one June day in 1892 had it slipped out of the wind's and the wave's way to this its final resting-place.

Now, in an age which is witnessing a renewed interest in its origins, it is perhaps time to retell the story of the *Beaver;* to give some account of its construction, launching, and long journey to this coast; to explain the part it was designed to take in the economic life of the area; to list some of the notable events in which it played a role; to sift, if we can, the fact from the fiction in the countless anecdotes which have gathered about it; and finally to estimate its importance in the development of the Pacific coast of British North America. Those who follow the *Beaver's* story to the end will surely agree that few ships — at least of those which have sailed these waters — have had a more varied career, or better deserve to be rescued from the obscurity which the accumulating years have laid upon it.

2 Tea kettles and beaver pelts

Sometime about the middle of the eighteenth century, a revolution commenced in human affairs which must be reckoned among the most important events in history. This was the substitution of machinery and steam for muscles as a means of doing work. Later, other sources of power would be found — oil, electricity, and eventually in our own day atomic energy; but steam, produced by burning coal, was first in the field, and as the decades went by, its effect on man's life, especially his economic life, became steadily more marked. From it resulted in due course the rise of the factory system, the growth of large industrial towns and the development of rapid transportation — in effect, the modern world.

No exact date can be given for what has been called with justice "the industrial revolution." As early as 1698 (that is, while people born in Shakespeare's lifetime were still living) Thomas Savery invented a machine for using the power of steam to raise water; in 1712 Thomas Newcomen, a blacksmith, devised what might be called a primitive steam-engine for pumping water out of coal mines; but the greatest share of the credit for making this new source of power available to mankind is usually assigned to James Watt (1737-1819). Tradition tells us that the idea first took shape in his mind when as a child he watched the rise and fall of the lid of a tea-kettle on the family stove. Regardless of the truth or falsity of this story, he eventually greatly improved Newcomen's invention, injecting steam both above and below the piston to drive it both up and down, and having patented his device, joined Matthew Boulton in 1774 in a partnership to manufacture engines for use in what was already a well-developed coal-mining industry. Soon, steam-engines were in use in cotton factories, iron and pottery works, paper mills and breweries. By 1800, there were perhaps three hundred such machines in existence, with a heavy concentration in the Lancashire cotton mills.[1]

With this increased use of steam came an expanded production of iron. Its smelting had previously required large quantities of charcoal, which as England became less wooded was difficult to obtain. Once coal was more easily available, the output of iron surged ahead, and there was soon a large production of it for export. (Bessemer's announcement in 1856 of a new means for converting iron into steel was to mark a further great advance, but this falls outside the period we are considering.)

Transportation was also soon revolutionized.

Charlotte Dundas, *1803, first steam-driven paddleship*

Roads and canals had been steadily improved throughout the eighteenth century, but September 27, 1825 saw the opening of a completely new era, as the Stockton and Darlington Railway began operations. All eyes were soon focused on the new invention when in 1829 George Stephenson, born in humble circumstances, achieved fame by producing his famous *Rocket,* which flashed through the English countryside between Liverpool and Manchester at the astronomical — by the standards of the day — speed of 29 miles an hour. Here indeed was a demonstration of the power of steam to reduce time and distance to manageable proportions.

Not only land but water transportation soon entered a new age. In 1786 William Symington, a Scot, patented a steam-engine for use in ships, but it was not until 1803 that a steam-driven ship, the *Charlotte Dundas,* first ran on the Forth and Clyde Canal. Quickly the new invention spread to the New World, as Robert Fulton secured engines from Boulton and Watt, and with them in 1807 drove a small vessel called the *Clermont* up the Hudson River from New York to Albany. The obvious advantages of steam over sail were quickly apparent, and numerous steam-driven vessels were soon plying between England, Ireland and France.

The broad ocean itself now witnessed the coming of the new force. The American ship *Savannah* used it as an auxiliary source of power when crossing the Atlantic from west to east in 1819. The first ship to cross the Atlantic entirely by steam, however, was apparently the Dutch vessel *Curaçao.* Built at Dover in 1826 and later renamed *Calpé,* this wooden paddle-steamer of 438 tons sailed from Rotterdam to the Dutch West Indies in April 1827, taking a month to make the voyage.

The first ship to make the voyage from the New World to the Old entirely by means of steam was, we may note, Canadian; this was the *Royal William,* built by Campbell and Black at Quebec in 1830/31 and launched on April 27 of the latter year. Its construction had been supervised by James Goudie, a Scotch-Canadian; although only 22, he had been to England and taken back to Canada the plans of the steamer *United Kingdom,* one of the pioneers of the run from London to Leith. The engines, made by Boulton and Watt, provided 200 horse-power for the 830-ton vessel. Leaving Quebec on August 5, 1833, and later Pictou, Nova Scotia on August 8, with seven passengers and a crew of thirty-six under Captain McDougall,

The Governor and Company of Adventurers of England Trading into Hudson's Bay, founded 1670

it reached Cowes on September 6 and Gravesend on September 12, in what was then considered a remarkably speedy crossing.

It was thus apparent by the time a third of the nineteenth century had gone by, that a new era in trade and transportation had begun; and this, as we shall see, was to have its effect on the policies of the powerful and complex organization founded in 1670 as "The Governor and Company of Adventurers of England trading into Hudson's Bay." We should now perhaps sketch in broadest outline the position of the HBC (as we may conveniently term it) as the nineteenth century began moving out into mid-stream.

The prospects of the Company were in fact highly promising, as a series of events had resulted in its enjoying a virtual monopoly of the fur trade throughout the northern half of North America.

This had not come, however, without a struggle. One competitor, the North West Company (founded in the winter of 1783/84) had in 1804 absorbed another, the XY Company, and a period of bitter rivalry with the HBC had then ensued, in which open violence was several times employed. Even this time of troubles, however, was marked by developments which in the long run were to consolidate the power of the HBC, as during it the North West Company established numerous posts throughout the West which later were to become part of the commercial network of the eventual victor in the struggle for control of the fur trade.

Among these were three founded by Simon Fraser or under his direction: Fort McLeod, the first trading-post west of the Rockies, founded in 1805; Fort St. James on Stuart Lake, built in 1806, and the oldest continuously settled community in what is now British Columbia; Fort George at the junction of the Nechako and Fraser Rivers, established in 1807. We may also note Kootenae House, the first trading-post in the Columbia basin, founded by David Thompson in the same year; Spokane House, built in 1810; Fort Okanogan, at the junction of the Okanogan and Columbia Rivers, founded by David Stuart in 1811; Kamloops, established in 1812 by J. J. Astor's fur company, and later taken over by the North West Company; Fort Walla Walla (Fort Nez Percés), founded in 1818; and Fort Alexandria (in what is now the Cariboo) established in 1821 by George McDougall and named in honor of Alexander Mackenzie, the first white man to reach the site.[2]

At these posts, furs were acquired from the

The combining of the fur companies

natives in exchange for baubles and blankets, and every spring the brigades were despatched on their long journey by canoe and pack-train to the eastern depots whence the furs were shipped to Europe (a number were sent by way of the mouth of the Columbia to China). In the fall, their long journey across half a continent completed, the brigades were back at the posts from which they had set out.

American competition was meanwhile nearly eliminated. A company headed by J. J. Astor had endeavored to establish a major outpost at the mouth of the Columbia River; it had founded Fort Astoria there in 1811, but Astor's grandiose plans for establishing a great network of trade stretching from Europe to Canton had ended in failure. During the war of 1812 the isolated garrison of this post decided to sell its buildings and supplies to the North West Company, and soon afterward H.M.S. *Racoon* took official possession of the post for England. The fort was restored to the United States under the eventual peace treaty, but Astor had lost interest in it, and the Northwesters remained in possession of the post, although the political future of the region as a whole — the "Oregon Territory" — was left to be settled by the governments of Britain and America at some future date.

The most important year in this period for the HBC, however, was undoubtedly 1821. In this year, the two major fur companies, weary of their long and unprofitable rivalry, decided to combine their forces. A merger was agreed upon, the resulting company was given the name of the older of its two constituents, and the North West Company thus disappeared from history.

This meant that the HBC not only had no serious competitors in any part of North America except Alaska, but also that it fell heir to the network of trading posts established by its former rival, as well as to their experienced personnel. To add to the Company's good fortune, it was granted by the British Government in the same year exclusive trading rights for 21 years in the vast area lying between the Great Lakes and the Rocky Mountains, as well as (for British subjects) in the "Oregon Territory" that lay between the Rockies and the Pacific Ocean. In this latter region, however, private American traders had the right to compete with the powerful British monopoly, as the political ownership of the area was still undetermined.

Even the sole remaining rival of the HBC, the Russian-American Fur Company, was soon to have

George Simpson takes control

bounds set to its ambitions. In 1812 it had established a post as far south as Bodega Bay, sixty-five miles north of San Francisco, but, perhaps influenced by President Monroe's enunciation in 1823 of his famous "doctrine", in 1824 agreed that 54° 40′ should be the southern limit of the Russian sphere of influence in North America. The following year saw the demarcation of what is now known as the "Alaskan Panhandle," British subjects being given the right for a period of ten years to trade in the coastal waters of this area and to make use of the port of Sitka.

By the end of the first quarter of the nineteenth century, then, it might fairly be said that the Hudson's Bay Company bestrode the northern half of North America like a colossus,[3] and one might have expected that it would now be content to enjoy its good fortune. Such, however, was far from the case, and we may ascribe this to three factors: the first was the tendency of any commercial organization to expand indefinitely until checked by some superior economic force; the second was the presence in the Company at many key posts in the field of unusually capable and energetic figures; and the third was the appointment in 1826 to the supreme direction of the Company's affairs in North America of probably the most remarkable figure in the history of the Company, George (later Sir George) Simpson.

Simpson had been born in Scotland in 1787.[4] Like James Douglas, that other towering figure in the Hudson's Bay Company during the middle years of the nineteenth century, he was illegitimate, but by virtue of a sound education and hard work had soon attracted the attention of his superiors. As early as 1820 Simpson had become deputy to William Williams, director of all HBC affairs in North America; in 1826 when Williams returned to England, Simpson succeeded to the position of Governor-in-chief, subject only to the Governor and Committee in London. Sometime between these two dates, however, Simpson had assumed effective control of all the Company's operations in the field.

A man of keen intellectual perception and tireless physical energy, he quickly set about the reorganization of the Company. As early as 1821 he was making lengthy tours of inspection of its posts on the prairies, and before long sending subordinates across the Rockies to examine the prospects of British Columbia — or, as it was then called, New Caledonia.

The regions to the west of the Great Divide,

indeed, soon gained his most zealous attention. Both New Caledonia and the "Columbia Department"—roughly, that area bounded by the 49th parallel to the north, the Rockies to the east, and Mexico to the south — had proved unprofitable to the North West Company, and the London management of the HBC were quite prepared, if Simpson so recommended, to abandon these regions. The latter, however, soon became convinced that with more capable direction they could be made to yield a good financial return to their new overlords.

Accordingly, once he had introduced efficiency into the main depots at Fort Garry and York Factory, he embarked on the remainder of his grand design. In August 1824, accompanied by Chief Trader James McMillan, eight voyageurs, an Indian guide and his personal servant, he set out by canoe on the long voyage to the Pacific coast. Before long he had overtaken a party headed by John McLoughlin, recently appointed Chief Factor of the Columbia Department, and the two groups went on together. At nearly every post along the way, Simpson found much that displeased him, and gave orders for improvements and economies. In October he crossed the Rockies and reached the upper waters of the Columbia, down which he travelled toward the sea. The local officials of the Company whom he encountered gave him bland assurances that all was well with its affairs, but this had scant effect on Simpson. As he noted in his journal:

> . . . if my information is correct, the Columbia Department from the day of its origin to the present hour has been neglected, shamefully mismanaged and a scene of the most wasteful extravagance and the most unfortunate dissention. It is high time the system should be changed and I think there is an ample field for reform and amendment.[5]

Simpson made changes in the personnel of some posts and ordered retrenchment in others; he then pressed on to the Pacific, reaching Fort George (the former Astoria) at the mouth of the Columbia twelve weeks after leaving York Factory, a record time for the journey.

Hardly had he arrived when he made important decisions. Suspecting that the fur trade would eventually be forced northward by the pressure of colonization from the eastern parts of the United States (though there was as yet no sign of this), he sent a party under Chief Trader James McMillan to explore the Fraser River with a view to opening a trade route from its mouth to the vast areas west of the Rockies. The suitability of the River was not

Fort Vancouver founded, 1825

determined on this occasion, but Simpson decided in any case to establish a new depot near its mouth, a decision which was to be put into effect with the construction of Fort Langley in 1827.

Simpson also stopped the supplying of liquor to the Indians, and ordered the construction of a new depot on the north bank of the Columbia, some eighty miles from its mouth. His reasoning was that this river might eventually be chosen as the boundary between British and American possessions, and though this did not prove to be the case when the boundary was finally settled under the Oregon Treaty of 1846, an important new post was quickly built, and on March 19, 1825 with considerable ceremony christened Fort Vancouver. Hardly had this been done when Simpson began his long journey back to Fort Garry, pounding dramatically on its gates at midnight on May 28.

In 1828 he was once more back in the Far West. Travelling in some state, no doubt to impress the Indians, he inspected numerous Company posts en route to the Pacific. Among them were Fort McLeod, where John Tod was in charge,[6] and Fort St. James, where in the absence of Chief Factor Connolly at Fort Vancouver he was received by Connolly's young assistant James Douglas.[7] From Kamloops, Simpson attempted to reach the coast by canoe, but found that both the Thompson and Fraser rivers were unnavigable. This convinced him that his previous idea of transferring the headquarters of the HBC on the Pacific coast from Fort Vancouver to the mouth of the Fraser was impractical, and that the Columbia would remain the main artery of the fur trade.

Simpson also in this period made some other far-reaching decisions. These were to participate more actively in the coastal trade (of which independent American traders were gaining a growing share), to establish a series of new posts along the North Pacific coast, and to connect this far-flung economic empire by means of a small fleet of trading-vessels. McLoughlin, in command of the Columbia Department, was not enthusiastic on this last point, but loyally set about putting the new policy into operation. In this he was to have almost a free hand, since Simpson was not to return to inspect the area until 1841.

Among the new posts founded as a result of Simpson's decisions were Fort Simpson, a little north of the present city of Prince Rupert, established in 1831 by Lt. Aemilius Simpson, R.N.,[8] and Peter Skene Ogden;[9] Fort McLoughlin on Milbanke

Men whose lives touched the 'Beaver'

James Watt (right), the man who powered the industrial revolution

Sir James Douglas (below, right), the founder of Fort Victoria and first Governor of British Columbia

John McLoughlin, Chief Factor of the HBC Columbia District at the time of the 'Beaver's' arrival on the west coast

Sir George Simpson, the dominant figure in the Hudson's Bay Company for over thirty years

Captain William H. McNeill (left), who commanded the 'Beaver' for many years

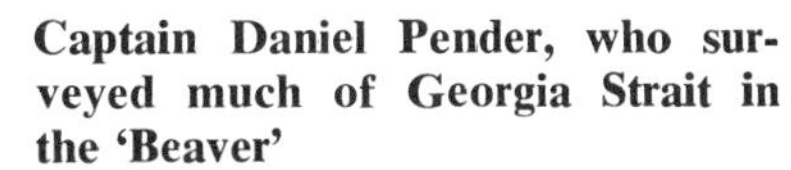

Captain Daniel Pender, who surveyed much of Georgia Strait in the 'Beaver'

Roderick Finlayson (below, left), Douglas' able second-in-command at the time of the founding of Fort Victoria

Captain George Marchant, veteran mariner and last captain of the 'Beaver'

A steamship — the master-stroke

Sound (near Bella Bella), founded in 1833, and Fort Nisqually on Puget Sound, founded the same year.[10]

The problem of shipping was still a vexatious one. The Company had a schooner, the *Broughton,* built on the Columbia in 1826, while in 1827 the brigantine *Cadboro* of 72 tons was purchased in England and sailed to Fort Vancouver by Captain John Pearson Swan; not long afterward it was put in charge of Aemilius Simpson. The loss of a single ship, however, could cause great inconvenience, and more than one was lost in this period. On March 10, 1829 the *William and Ann,* under the command of Captain Swan, was wrecked on the Columbia River bar, and its crew killed by Indians, while the next year the *Isabella* was lost in the same place. In 1831 the 85-ton schooner *Vancouver* (built on the Columbia River in 1826) ran aground and was badly damaged.[11]

Faced with these set-backs, and keenly aware of the persistent and often successful American competition in the North Pacific, Simpson now decided on a master-stroke. Sailing vessels were often at the mercy of winds and tides, but a ship powered by steam might successfully evade these dangers, and soon establish the commercial supremacy of the HBC throughout the area. Accordingly on August 10, 1832 he wrote to his superiors in London, outlining his new plan:

> The advantages which a Steam Vessel would possess over sailing craft in navigating the rivers inlets and sounds, which are so numerous on that coast, and where all the trade is made, embolden us to request that Your Honors will be pleased to provide a Vessel of that description. We are aware that the first cost would be heavy, but we feel assured that she would, in a very short time, become the cheapest craft that could be used, and perform more effective service than any two Sailing Vessels which might be provided.
>
> The saving of time in ascending and descending the Columbia and Fraser's Rivers of itself would be a very important object, as it rarely happens that any of the craft we now have perform the trip between Cape Disappointment and Vancouver in less than three weeks — while the river is high, which, with the detention at Bakers Bay and off the mouth of the river from calms and head winds, occasion a prodigious loss of time; indeed a Vessel entering the Columbia, and having occasion to go up to Vancouver, cannot be expected to get to sea again in less than a couple of months, and craft have been known to be windbound in Baker's Bay for six weeks

at a time, being unable to work over the bar.

Much valuable time is likewise lost in ascending Fraser's river to Fort Langley owing to the strength of the current when the water is high and calms; and at Nass there will likewise be a considerable loss of time in working out and in to the Establishment; indeed it is ascertained that a Vessel can perform the voyage from the Port of Nass to the Sandwich Islands and back again in less time than from Nass to Vancouver and back.

A steam Vessel would afford us incalculable advantages over the Americans, as we could look into every Creek and cove while they were confined to a harbour by head winds and calms, we could ascend every stream of any consequence upon the coast, we could visit our establishments at stated periods, in short a Steam Vessel would, in our opinion, bring the contest to a close very soon, by making us masters of the trade.

The Vessel we require should not exceed 180 tons burden, and be of small draft of water, to enable her to run into the different rivers; the machinery of the very best description, with two working engineers; and a respectable well conducted man to navigate her, with two steady active able bodied mates. Machinery is now brought to such perfection that with good management accidents rarely occur, but in order to guard against accident it would be well to have a double set of such parts of the machinery as are most likely to give way, and by that means, as we have forges and blacksmiths at every establishment on the coast, we could make such repairs as might be necessary from time to time.

It would of course be necessary to send the machinery as cargo, as the voyage from England is too long to be attempted by steam, and the rigging stores etc. could either be applied to another sailing vessel of the same size, after she had performed the voyage from England, or used in addition to the steam machinery. We have no idea what the cost of such a Vessel might be, but should not consider her too expensive at about £6,000.[12]

McLoughlin, however, though in fact as early as 1826 (and again in 1827) he had remarked to Simpson on the possible benefits to be derived from a steamer,[13] was not at this time in accordance with Simpson's views, and the next year outlined his own for the benefit of the Governor and Committee in London:

And as to employing a Steam Boat I have no data to give me an idea of the Cost of such a Vessel, but in my opinion they are very expensive; it is true they are the most convenient Vessels we could have on the Coast,

The order is placed

> but at present with the number of Vessels we have I am of opinion we ought not to open a new Channel of expense, and next year if the Americans do not return, I would reduce the Establishment of Vessel to two and remove Ft. Simpson to Dundas Island as Mr. Finlayson suggests or to Stikine if found practicable.[14]

The ultimate authorities of the HBC, however, decided in favor of Simpson, and so informed him in a letter dated March 5, 1834:

> The steam Vessel about to be sent out will be expensive, but she will possess so many advantages over sailing craft on the Coast, which from its broken character, and the protection afforded by Islands render it peculiarly well adapted for Steam navigation, so that this Vessel, altho costly in the first instance, will soon be productive of a considerable saving, as she is expected to perform the service of four of the Sailing Vessels now employed on the Coast. . . . [15]

The Company also soon afterwards wrote to Boulton and Watt, giving specifications as to the type of engines they required:

> . . . I am now to request you will put in hand forthwith, the Two 35 Horse power Engines, with Boiler capable of burning wood or best Coal; the duplicate tools Stores etc etc as p specification handed the 16th Inst. the same to be delivered at Messrs Green & Wigrams Yard Blackwall as early as possible say within five months of the present time.
>
> I am further to mention that Messrs Green & Wigrams are now raising the frame of the Vessel for which the Engines are intended, and I am to request you will consult with them as to where the Paddle Boxes should be placed, and on all other matters connected with the proper fixing of the Engines.[16]

And so it was that the decision was made which within two years was to bring the *Beaver* to the Pacific Coast, there to begin its long and varied career first for the HBC, later for the Royal Navy, and finally for private local owners. Trading vessel, survey ship, warship; at one time or another it would be each of these. Moreover, whenever in the middle years of the century important deeds were afoot, or much was to hang in the balance, there the sturdy little craft would play her part. It will soon be apparent as the story of these years is told that no account of the next half century on Canada's Pacific coast can be written which is not inextricably interwoven with the name of S.S. *Beaver*.

Footnotes

[1] It is believed that the first issue of a newspaper printed on a steam-operated press was the *Times* of Nov. 29, 1814. The press was built by Frederick Koenig, a Saxon.

[2] Fort Alexandria was originally built on the east bank of the Fraser, about 35 miles south of the modern town of Quesnel. In 1836 it was moved to the west bank of the Fraser. It was abandoned as a trading post about 1880. See Morice, A. G., *The History of the Northern Interior of British Columbia,* Toronto, 1904, pp. 44, 122, 194.

[3] "At the height of its expansion, the Company ruled an area of more than 3,000,000 square miles, approximately one-fourth of the continent of North America" (J. S. Galbraith, *The Hudson's Bay Company as an Imperial Factor, 1821-1869,* U. of Toronto Press, 1957, p. 3). To manage the economic life of this huge area, the Company had in the mid-1830's a grand total of 1294 employees (*ibid.,* p. 21).

[4] This, at least, is the date on his tombstone, though the *Dictionary of National Biography* gives it as 1792. Simpson himself was extremely reticent regarding his background. We might note that like many others employed by the fur trade in North America during this period, he had several illegitimate children, whom he acknowledged and for whom he made financial provision. (See J. S. Galbraith, *Op. Cit.,* and also his article "The Little Emperor" in the *Beaver* for Winter 1960; also Douglas Mackay, *The Honourable Company,* McClelland and Stewart, Toronto, 1936, p. 198.) Simpson had a ready rationalization for this custom: "Since connubial alliances are the best security we can have of the goodwill of natives, I have therefore recommended the Gentlemen to form connections with the principal families immediately upon their arrival . . . This is no difficult matter, as the offer of their Wives & daughters is the first token of their Friendship & hospitality." (Frank Rasky: *The Taming of the Canadian West,* McClelland and Stewart, 1967, p. 115.)

[5] *Fur Trade and Empire: George Simpson's Journal,* ed. Frederick Merk, Harvard University Press, 1968, p. 43.

[6] Tod was born in Scotland in 1793 or 1794, and entered the service of the HBC about 1811. He became a member of the first Legislative Council of Vancouver Island, appointed by Governor Blanshard in 1851. He died in Victoria on August 31, 1882. His amatory alliances were of bewildering complexity, a valiant effort being made to disentangle them in an article by Madge Wolfenden in the *BCHQ* for July-Oct. 1954, pp. 231-238. See also my *James Douglas: Servant of Two Empires* (Mitchell Press, Vancouver, 1969, pp. 15-16). Tod's house, built in 1851, is the oldest in Victoria (2564 Heron St., Oak Bay). See the article on it in the *Beaver* for June 1948.

[7] Douglas was born in 1803, probably in the vicinity of Demarara, in British Guiana, the illegitimate son of John Douglas, a Scottish businessman, and an unknown mother. Educated in Scotland, he joined the North West Company and in 1819 sailed for the New World. Here he was posted successively at Fort William, Isle-à-la-crosse (in what is now northern Saskatchewan), Fort McLeod and Fort St. James. He married Connolly's half-breed daughter Amelia (1812-1890), by whom he had thirteen children, and who eventually became Lady Douglas.

[8] Aemilius Simpson entered the Royal Navy in 1806, became a lieutenant, and retired on half-pay in December, 1816. In 1826 he was appointed a hydrographer-surveyor at £150 per annum. He arrived at Fort Vancouver on November 2, 1826. When the *Cadboro* arrived there in 1827 he was put in charge of her, remaining in charge until 1831, when he was given the

Dryad. On November 3, 1830 he was made a Chief Trader. In the summer of 1831 he established a post at the mouth of the Nass River; here he died on September 13, 1831 after a brief illness. Three years later when this post was removed to Dundas Island and named Fort Simpson in his honor, his body was taken there for burial. He was distantly related to Sir George Simpson. See *Minutes of the Council of the Northern Department of Rupert's Land, 1821-1831,* ed. R. H. Fleming, Toronto, the Champlain Society, 1940, p. 454.

[9] Ogden had an interesting background. His father, Isaac, had left the United States when the American Revolution proved successful, and later held various judicial positions in Canada. Peter Skene Ogden, born in 1794, entered the service of the North West Company some time between 1809 and 1811, but his services were dispensed with when the union with the HBC took place in 1821. Later, however, the HBC employed him in the Columbia Department, from whence he led several expeditions into the interior of the continent between 1824 and 1830. He eventually rose to the rank of Chief Factor, and died September 27, 1854 at Oregon City. Ogden Point, Victoria, is named after him. See Galbraith, *Op. Cit.,* pp. 89-94.

[10] There is an interesting article on Fort Nisqually in the HBC magazine *Beaver* for Summer 1961.

[11] This ship should not be confused with the barque *Vancouver* (400 tons), built of teak for the HBC by Messrs. Green, Wigrams and Green of Blackwall in 1838. While in command of Captain Mouat, it was wrecked while entering the Columbia River on May 7, 1848. Its officers and crew were saved but the Columbia supplies for 1849 were lost. See Lewis and Dryden, *Marine History of the Pacific Northwest,* ed. E. W. Wright, Antiquarian Press, New York, 1961, p. 24; also J. R. Anderson, Notes and Comments (unpublished MS in PABC) p. 189.

[12] Simpson to Governor and Committee, dated York Factory, August 10, 1832. This letter is made available by kind permission of the present Governor and Committee.

[13] *Letters of John McLoughlin, 1st series, 1825-1838,* ed. E. E. Rich, Toronto, the Champlain Society, 1941, p. lxxiv.

[14] McLoughlin to Governor and Committee, August 31, 1833, *ibid.,* p. 111.

[15] Governor and Committee to Simpson, March 5, 1834. Quoted in W. K. Lamb, "The Advent of the Beaver", *BCHQ,* July 1938, p. 167.

[16] Extract from a letter from Secretary William Smith, Hudson's Bay Company, to Messrs. Boulton Watt & Co., Soho, dated London, September 20, 1834. This extract has been made available by the kind permission of the Governor and Committee of the Hudson's Bay Company.

3 First smokestack in the northeast Pacific

Once the decision had been made by the directors of the HBC to build a steamship for service on the Pacific coast, every care was taken to see that the vessel would perform its duties with success. The materials of which it was built were the most durable that could be found, and its construction was unusually sturdy. The ship, rated at 109 tons, was 100′ 9″ long and 20 feet wide (or 33 feet, including the paddle-boxes); the depth of its hold was 11 feet, and its draught when loaded was about eight and a half feet. The paddle-wheels were thirteen feet in diameter, with paddles six and a half feet long which revolved, when at top speed, at thirty times a minute. It had two masts and a single tall funnel, while only a small bridge rose above the gunwale.[1]

Charles McCain, who wrote a history of the vessel in 1894, gave a detailed account of its mode of construction, and we cannot perhaps do better than quote extensively from it:

> The elm keel was of unusual size and strength as was also the British oak stem and stern-post. Along the keel were placed the frames, or ribs, at about 2 feet centres. These were of the best oak and greenheart, carefully dressed and of large proportions. The spaces between the frames were filled in solid, to a level above the water line, with curved timbers of the same material and thickness. The outside planking was of oak and African teak, especially thick at the wales, and was securely fastened to the frames with copper bolts and oak treenails. This was covered with a thick layer of tarred paper, over which was placed a planking of fir, securely held in position with spikes of a bronze composition. Then to preserve the woodwork from the ravages of the destructive teredo, and also from the attacks of barnacles, a sheathing of copper was tack-fastened all over the exterior of the hull, with the exception of a narrow strip just below the gunwale. The inside lining of the frame consisted also of oak and teak planking, across which on either side ran diagonally heavy iron straps, which were fastened to the frames with rivetted copper bolts.
>
> The main keelson was a massive stick of greenheart, 12 inches square, extending the entire length of the keel, to which it was securely bolted with stout copper bolts, which passed entirely through both timbers. Parallel to this, on either side, were the sister keelsons, of the same material, only not quite so heavy; these were also bolted in a substantial manner on the floor planks, and through into the floor timbers. Across the keelsons were fastened large greenheart timbers, which formed

The Beaver's *first engines*

> the bed for the engines as well as the foundation for the furnaces. The deck was supported by a series of stout beams, mostly of greenheart, the remainder being African oak, or, as it is more commonly called, African teak. These were placed at frequent intervals across the hull, to which they were fastened, their supports being oak knees and massive angle irons. In addition to these were two oak beams, about 10 inches by 14, which crossed at the points where the two spars penetrated the deck.[2]

McCain also gives some details of the ship's engines:

> These engines, of which there were two of the same design, were termed 35 nominal horsepower each, and were of the side-lever type, which, in the earliest experiments of steam marine navigation, was the style universally favored; but this has long since become obsolete.
>
> The cylinders stood vertical and had a diameter of 42 inches, with a 36-inch stroke. The piston-rod projected through the top of the cylinder to the centre of a sliding crosshead, at the ends of which linked rods ran down on either side of the cylinder to a pair of horizontal beams, or levers, which oscillated on a fixed gudgeon at the middle of their length. The opposite ends of these beams were joined by means of a crosstail, from which connecting rods led up to the crank shaft above. This shaft, six inches in diameter, was in three sections, and was thus supplied with four cranks, each of which was 18 inches in length. At each extremity of the outer portions of this shaft was a paddle-wheel 13 feet in diameter, made up of 11 radial arms 5 feet in width.
>
> The low-pressure boiler, which rested on brick furnaces, and from which steam was carried through large copper tubes to the steam chests, was situated about midship, but still some distance aft of the engines. This arrangement crowded the paddle-wheels far forward, like the fins of a seal, thus giving the little steamer a very unique appearance.[3]

Some controversy has arisen as to the pressure which the ship's boilers could develop. Some writers have stated that the working pressure of the *Beaver's* boilers was only 2½ pounds to the square inch, while others have asserted that the vessel could not have run at all in that case. It is hard to determine the exact truth of the matter, but the pressure was undoubtedly very low, as one old-timer who remembered the steamer declared that the ship was unable to blow its whistle while in motion.

The launching by Mrs. John Labouchere

Work on the vessel proceeded methodically, and on May 2, 1835 it was ready to be launched. There was not, as has been frequently stated, a large crowd at the ceremony, nor was King William the Fourth among the spectators. Nevertheless, the customary rites were duly carried out, and the vessel was christened by Mrs. John Labouchere, sister-in-law of Henry Labouchere, vice-president of the London Board of Trade.

On June 25, its fitting out completed, the *Beaver* went for a trial cruise in the English Channel. All went well, and the engines were then dismantled and the paddlewheels unshipped, as it had been decided that the actual journey to the Pacific coast should be made by sail and not entrusted to the new method of propulsion.

In the meantime, another vessel was also being built for the Company; the barque *Columbia* of 310 tons, which, also built at the yard of Green, Wigrams and Green, was launched on July 8, 1835. It was designed for use as the annual supply ship for the northwest coast, carrying there goods unprocurable in that region and bringing back furs to Europe.

It was intended that the *Beaver* and the *Columbia* should travel to the Pacific in company, and accordingly the two vessels left Gravesend on August 27. The *Columbia* was under the command of Captain William Darby, while Captain David Home, formerly of the East India Company's service, had been selected as the first captain of the *Beaver*. Other members of the *Beaver's* crew were:

1st officer	W. C. Hamilton
2nd officer	Charles Dodd
Chief engineer	Peter Arthur
Second engineer	John Donald
Carpenter	Henry Barrett
Able seamen	William Wilson
	George Gordon
	William Phillips
	James Dick
	George Holland
	James McIntyre
	William Burns

Although most of the logs kept during the *Beaver's* later career have most regrettably been lost, a copy of the log kept during its journey to the Pacific coast has survived, and we have thus a detailed record of its long voyage from the old world to the new.[4] Early in September the *Columbia* reported to the *Beaver* the death of Mr. Carney, its chief mate. A few days later the

Rounding the Horn

log notes: "Light airs and rain. People employed about the rigging, sixty gallons of water expended, 4,072 remaining." On September 11 we find "people employed washing clothes and airing bedding," while the next day they were "employed scrubbing paint work, cleaning 'tween decks and greasing masts." For September 13, the log notes: "Read prayers to the ship's company"; on this day the two vessels reached Madeira.

The weather, at first good, soon deteriorated, for on September 26 there was "heavy rain with thunder and lightning; weather too unsettled to say prayers." The storm evidently drove at least one of the ships off course, for they lost sight of each other, and on September 30 the *Beaver* "fired three rockets for the *Columbia* but received no answer."

Proceeding separately, the *Beaver* reached Trinidad on October 15. The weather evidently was not much improved, for on October 25 it was still "too unsettled to read prayers." On November 11 the *Beaver* reached the Falkland Islands, and on November 18 Cape Horn, which was safely rounded. On November 25 "a sudden squall carried away top mast steering sail boom," and there was a "heavy fall of snow." On November 27 there was still a "strong gale and heavy sea," and the ship was "lying to under double-reefed foresail." On December 12 the *Beaver* reached the Island of Juan Fernandez, due west of Valparaiso, Chile, and the next day anchored in Cumberland Harbor. From here on December 17, 1835, Captain Home wrote informing the London management of the HBC that "the *Beaver* is an excellent sea-boat, and should the engines go wrong will answer as a sailing vessel perfectly well."[5] Soon the *Columbia* appeared, and on December 18 the two ships set sail together for the Sandwich Islands.

On the day before Christmas, the *Columbia* "sent a boat aboard for fresh beef." The same day the *Beaver* requested a doctor, as the first mate, W. C. Hamilton, was ill. The *Columbia's* doctor, however, sent word that he himself was too ill to come. No more, though, is recorded of these matters.

On the fourth of February, the ships came to anchor at Honolulu, and the crews went ashore. One of them, William Wilson of the *Beaver,* did so without leave, and Captain Home considered having him left behind; however, "William Wilson showing great contrition for his offence and the rest of the people begging that he be not punished, and that they would be answerable for his conduct in the

Safely anchored at Fort Vancouver

future, I reprimanded him and sent him to his duty."

On February 19 the log notes that the *Beaver* "let the old stock of water out of the boilers, it being very bad. Took on board 1000 gallons of water." On February 25 the ships set sail. Two changes were first made in their personnel: four Sandwich Islanders were taken on board the *Columbia* to work their passage to North America,[6] and Charles Dodd, second officer of the *Beaver* (and one day to be its captain) exchanged places with Mr. Prattent, who held the same position on the *Columbia.*

The two ships again lost sight of each other as they neared the American coast, which was reached in mid-March. However, they did re-establish contact, and both were soon anchored at Fort George at the mouth of the Columbia. On March 25 a pilot arrived from Fort Vancouver to pilot the *Beaver* up the river, accompanied by the *Columbia.* The latter on one occasion ran aground, but the *Beaver* sent a boat to assist in freeing her, and the two ships then continued their voyage. On April 10, 1836 they anchored safely at Fort Vancouver; the long voyage across half the world was over.

Little time, however, was wasted in celebrating the achievement. The installation of the *Beaver's* engines and paddle-wheels began at once, and on May 16 its log notes: "At 4 p.m. the engineers got the steam up and tried the engines and found (them) to answer very well."

The *Beaver* was next tested on short runs, as the log notes:

> Tuesday, May 17 at daylight unmoored ship and got the steam up. At 3:30 weighed and ran down abreast of the lower plain for fire-wood. At noon lashed alongside the *Columbia.* At 1:30 took the *Columbia* in tow up to the saw-mill. At 6 returned and anchored off Fort Vancouver in 5 fathoms. Received the 9 lb. long gun from the *Columbia.*

Several other short trial runs were made, some of which were evidently "sight-seeing tours," for we find that on "May 31 at 9:30 a party of ladies and gentlemen from the fort came on board." We are lucky in having the impressions of one of the *Beaver's* first passengers. His name was Samuel Parker, and in recording his experiences he put a prophetic finger unerringly on the significance of this new phenomenon in waters which had hitherto seen only sails:

> The novelty of a steamboat on the Columbia

> awakened a train of prospective reflections upon the probable changes which would take place in these remote regions in a very few years. It was wholly an unthought of thing when I first contemplated this enterprise (i.e. his journey across North America—Ed.) that I should find here this forerunner of commerce and business. The gaiety which prevailed was often suspended while we conversed of coming days when with civilized men, all the rapid improvements in the arts of life should be introduced over this new world, and when cities and villages shall spring up on the west, as they are springing up on the east of the great mountains, and a new empire be added to the kingdoms of the earth.[7]

It might be well at this point to note that the *Beaver* was not, as has often been stated, "the first steamer in the Pacific." The Pacific is a large ocean, and other corners of it had already seen the coming of steam. The first ship to use it in the Pacific was, so far as is known, the *Telica,* a Spanish paddle-steamer, which was active in the waters of Mexico and Central America (and perhaps came as far north as San Francisco) as early as 1825. Its career was, however, short-lived, as its captain committed suicide by blowing up the ship's cargo of gunpowder. Australian waters saw a steamship a few years later. The 250-ton paddle-steamer *Sophia Jane* left London in December 1830 and reached Sydney, New South Wales, on May 14, 1831. Like the *Beaver,* it made the voyage under sail, with its engines stowed on board. The enterprising Australians themselves soon built a steam-driven craft. this was the *Surprise,* launched in Sydney in 1831 and designed for service on the Paramatta River. It was far from speedy, however, being able to manage only 4½ knots, and after a few years service in Tasmanian waters, its engines were removed, and the vessel became the schooner *Anna Jane.* Another early steamship was the *Tamar.* This craft, of 140 tons, with engines developing 60 horse-power, was built in Glasgow and arrived (under sail) in Tasmanian waters in September 1834. Its career was to be a long and useful one, only ending when it was wrecked in 1873.[8]

So far as is known, however, these four ships were the *Beaver's* only predecessors in the vast Pacific, and certainly the northwest coast of America had seen no steam-driven vessel before the *Beaver's* arrival there in 1836.

The HBC's new acquisition had been tested as a steamer on the waters of the Columbia; now it was time to venture into the great ocean itself.

First voyage up the northwest coast

Setting out on June 19 (it apparently never saw the Columbia again), it took on board Chief Factor Duncan Finlayson[9] and then moved up the west coast of the continent. Captain Home was in command, Charles Dodd was first mate and Alexander Lattie second mate. The crew numbered 31, including four stokers and thirteen wood-cutters, many of them Kanakas or Indians. Some of the events of the next few weeks are told in the laconic language of the ship's log:

> June 19 at 5 a.m. weighed and ran down the river. At 6:30 very hazy, and not being able to see the channel, anchored opposite Gray's Bay village. At 7:45 weighed, and at 8:45 grounded on the east sand in Tongue Point channel. Endeavored to back her off, but the tide ebbing very fast found it impossible; ran a kedge out and waited for the flood. At 3 p.m. with the assistance of a boat's crew from the *Columbia* we hove off and ran through the channel. At 4:30 anchored in Baker's Bay in company with the *Columbia;* found the engines to work extremely well. Draught of water 9-6 forward, 10-6 aft. Laid in the bay until 26th, getting wood, etc. and waiting for the swell to subside. June 26th at 1 p.m. weighed anchor and ran towards the bar. At 2 crossed the bar, the least water being quarter less four. At 2:30 Cape Disappointment bore N.E. by E. at 5.15 E. by S. ½ E. At 11 p.m. the planking in the deck cabins began giving away in a cross sea, carpenter securing them. June 27 the after part of the starboard paddle-box carried away. At daylight saw the high land to the N. of Nootka Sound. June 28 running along the land. At daylight saw Scot's Island on the starboard bow. June 29 finding that we had not enough fuel to carry us to Millbank Fort, stopped the steam and made sail to the topsail and unshipped five paddle-blades, made steam and entered Millbank Sound, anchoring at 11 in 10 fathoms. June 30 at 4, after taking on a supply of wood, weighed and ran up to the Sound, anchored at 6:30 opposite Millbank fort, saluted the fort with seven guns, which were returned. Arrived at Fort Simpson, being 6 days going up, owing to frequent stops for wood. July 14 arrived at Tungase and found there the Russian Fur Company's brig *Chitsekoff.*[10]

At Tungase (or Tongass) a Russian officer came on board the *Beaver* and told Finlayson that the ship was forbidden to travel to Sitka by way of the interior channels. Finlayson replied through the interpreter that a convention previously drawn up by the two great fur companies, the HBC and the Russian-American Company, permitted such a voyage. Agreement not being reached, the *Beaver* then returned to Fort Simpson, and not long afterward Finlayson, travelling in the *Llama*, interviewed the Russian governor at Sitka, when various matters in dispute were amicably settled.

We might note that Finlayson was already in no doubt as to the value of the *Beaver,* reporting to McLoughlin that:

> On the whole she will give the most effectual blow to the opposition which they have ever met with off the coast, and will also lessen in a great measure the traffic carried on amongst the natives themselves.[11]

Finlayson evidently had in mind the activities of independent American traders, who, since the *Beaver* could call at any place desired along the coast, would now find the search for furs much more difficult.

There were other promising results of this first expedition of the *Beaver*. Its successful deep penetration of the coastal inlets had shown how superior its motive power was to reliance on the winds and tides. A fair number of furs had been collected, considering that the year was already well advanced; moreover, it had been confirmed that there were coal deposits on northern Vancouver Island at a point approximately 50° 30′ N. and 126° 35′ W., and natives had been promised payment for digging it. In the meantime samples were collected for forwarding to England for analysis, while Finlayson envisaged in his report to McLoughlin both a mine and a fort in this area:

> The Indians informed us that at a considerable distance behind this place, there is a mountain of pure coal. But I am sorry to observe that I do not think the mine can be worked without building an Establishment at it, there being a very populous village of Quaquill Indians, consisting of from 50 to 60 houses within 2½ miles of it, and purchasing the mine from them would be of little use, as the people left to work it would, unless protected by a large force, be exposed to the attacks of other tribes who frequent this spot. I would therefore consider the mine without the protection of a Fort, useless to us.[12]

The *Beaver* had thus already begun to play a part in the economic development of the Pacific coast. Moreover, it had also had a considerable effect in the more shadowy realm of the intangible. The Indians were greatly impressed with the fire-breathing monster, declaring that the white man must have been aided in its construction by the Great Spirit. Though they may never have heard the saying that

The Beaver *meets its first challenge!*

imitation is the sincerest form of flattery, their admiration soon took them as far as attempting to duplicate it. A large tree, some twenty to thirty feet long, was modelled into the approximate shape of the *Beaver,* painted black and decked over, while bright red paddles were constructed. Its motive power, however, was supplied not by Messrs. Boulton and Watt but by concealed Indian braves who turned the paddles by sheer muscle-power. Despite this prompt challenge to the white man's supremacy, the dark-skinned warriors failed to wrest the riband of these narrow seas from Captain Home, their greatest exertions propelling their craft at only three miles an hour.[13]

That the *Beaver* had some drawbacks, however, was evident even this early. It was not always able to give its passengers a smooth journey, Finlayson reporting to McLoughlin that:

> Our progress was much impeded by the steamer's being so heavily laden, the paddles sometimes plunging into the waves which shook the vessel much, and in a very heavy sea I would consider a vessel under sail as the safest mode of conveyance.[14]

The *Beaver* also required remarkable amounts of fuel. In order to travel for a day (perhaps 90 miles) the ship had to stop for two days while its wood-cutters cut down trees and made cord-wood of them. Its average progress was thus not more than 30 miles per day, though when wood was already available at a post, this could of course be exceeded.

Following this initial trip into northern waters, the *Beaver* returned to Fort Nisqually. Before long, though, it had once again gone as far as Fort Simpson, where it spent its first winter on the Pacific coast.

Already, however, it had accomplished much. It had successfully made its way across half the globe to take part in the opening of this distant and largely still undeveloped part of the world; even in its first few months of service, it had added to man's knowledge of the area; while its turning paddles had signalled that the days of sail must give way to those of steam.[15] The mists of time, in fact, were receding, and silhouetted against the rising sun of the new day would be the smoke-stack of the *Beaver.* Its engines were weak indeed compared with those which these waters would some day know, but their sound was in some ways louder; it was the heart-beat of the modern age.

Footnotes

[1] W. K. Lamb, "The Advent of the Beaver", *BCHQ,* Vol. II, No. 3, July 1938.

[2] Charles McCain, *History of the S.S. Beaver,* Vancouver, B.C., 1894, p. 16.
Greenheart is a tree found in British Guiana, and growing to a height of 75 to 100 feet. It is very heavy, but almost immune to teredos.
The teak of the *Beaver* had probably been cut in India and taken to England by sailing ship.

[3] *Ibid.,* p. 18.

[4] It may be found in Lewis and Dryden's *Marine History of the Pacific Northwest,* ed. E. W. Wright, Antiquarian Press, New York, 1961, pp. 15-17.
Holland Point, off Dallas Road, Victoria, is named after George Holland, a member of the *Beaver's* first crew. See *BCHQ,* Vol. XVIII, 1954, pp. 117-121.

[5] See Lamb, W. K., "The Advent of the *Beaver", BCHQ,* July 1938, p. 170.
Juan Fernandez is sometimes called "Robinson Crusoe Island", as the famous work by Daniel Defoe is based on the adventures of Alexander Selkirk, who was shipwrecked and lived alone there from 1704 to 1709. There is a memorial to him on the island.

[6] There was a small but steady movement of Sandwich Islanders, or Kanakas, to the Northwest during this period. Little trace now remains of them, but Kanaka Bay, Esquimalt and Kanaka Bar on the Fraser are reminders of them. Humboldt Street, Victoria, was originally known as Kanaka Row. Hawaiians were amongst the first settlers on Salt Spring Island where their descendants are an identifiable part of the modern population. (See *Salt Spring Island* by Bea Hamilton, Mitchell Press, Vancouver, 1969, pp. 77-85.)

[7] Parker, S., *Journal of an exploring tour beyond the Rocky Mountains,* 2nd edition, Ithaca, New York, 1840, p. 314.

[8] For material on these early steamships, see "First steamers on the Pacific", by Capt. P. A. McDonald, in *Nautical Research Journal,* Whittier, California, Vol. 3, No. 11, November 1951.

[9] Duncan Finlayson was the uncle of Roderick Finlayson, in charge of Fort Victoria from 1844 to 1849.

[10] Lewis and Dryden, *Op. Cit.,* p. 17.
Fort Tongass, on Tongass Island (54° 46′ N., 130° 35′ W.) was about three miles east of Cape Fox and 16 miles northwest of Port Simpson. It became an American possession after the purchase of Alaska from Russia in 1867, and a post was maintained there for a time. It was justly considered a wet, dreary place. The *Beaver* visited it again in 1868.

[11] Duncan Finlayson to McLoughlin, 29 September 1836. *Letters of John McLoughlin,* first series, Toronto, The Champlain Society, 1941, p. 328.

[12] Duncan Finlayson to McLoughlin, Sept. 29, 1836. *Letters to John McLoughlin,* first series, p. 335.

[13] John Dunn, *History of the Oregon Territory and British North American Fur Trade,* London, 1844, pp. 271-272. Dunn served for a time in the brig *Cadboro*; he is buried in the Sandwich (Hawaiian) Islands. One of his daughters, Elizabeth, married Captain Thomas Pamphlet, at one time master of the *Beaver.* Their son, Captain Frederick William Pamphlet, born in Victoria in 1871, also had a distinguished career, including the command of the S.S. *Badger.* He died at the age of 80 in the North Vancouver General Hospital on Nov. 10, 1951.

[14] Duncan Finlayson to McLoughlin, Sept. 29, 1836. *Letters of John McLoughlin,* first series, p. 327.

[15] It is interesting to note that on the other side of British North America the transition to modern times was proceeding almost simultaneously. The first Canadian steam railway, the Champlain and St. Lawrence, was opened on July 23, 1836.

The 'Beaver' proves its worth

1836 had seen the *Beaver* begin to play its part in joining the scattered outposts of civilization in the northwest; the next year would see it give further good service in this cause. It was also to receive a new master, as Captain Home was succeeded by Captain William Henry McNeill.

The *Beaver's* first captain had performed his duties efficiently, but apparently wished for more tangible recognition of the fact. According to a letter written by John McLoughlin, in charge of all HBC operations on the Pacific coast, Captain Home had asked to be advanced to the rank of "Chief Trader." McLoughlin felt unable to accede to this promotion, and offered the captain instead an increase in salary. This was not satisfactory to Home, who declared he would not remain in the Company's service unless given the title he coveted. McLoughlin would not agree to this request, though he was quite ready to go on record as considering Home "a steady good officer fit for any command in our navy".[1] Accordingly, Captain Home resigned and his place was taken by McNeill.

McNeill was probably born in Boston in 1803.[2] As early as 1823 he was a master mariner, and in 1825 was on the northwest coast in command of the brig *Convoy,* trading with the Indians of the area. The log of this vessel for this period is in the Provincial Archives, Victoria, and gives us some idea of McNeill's activities. We learn, for example, that the brig was owned by "Josiah Marshall, merchant of Boston," and that it left that port in October 1824, rounding Cape Horn at the end of the year, and reaching Juan Fernandez Island in February 1825. Here four of the crew, including the sailmaker and carpenter, deserted and could not be found. Nothing daunted, McNeill took on fresh water and fruit, and sailed for Hawaii where he sold cloth and hardware to the natives. He then set sail for the northwest coast of America, reaching the Queen Charlotte Islands in April. Here he traded with the Indians for furs, which included 260 valuable sea otters. Not everything went smoothly on board the *Convoy,* however, for in October 1825 various members of the crew "made use of mutinous language." This apparently did not dismay McNeill, for the log merely notes that "the forecastle was then closed upon them and half a pint water and half a biscuit per day for each man was ordered for their allowance," and there are no further references to the affair. On January 2, 1826, however, while the vessel was in the Hawaiian Islands, there was again trouble, and we learn that "the steward after giving abusive language and quarrelling with the crew was flogged and sent on shore."

McNeill's activities for the next few years are not known in detail, but in 1831 he was again on the Pacific coast, this time as master of the brig *Llama*. This vessel, 144 tons and 76 feet long, was owned by the Boston firm of Bryant and Sturgis. McNeill made numerous trading voyages in it, touching at places as widely separated as Tahiti, Samoa, Hawaii, New Zealand, and, on Vancouver Island, Quatsino, Kyuquot and Barclay Sound. Puget Sound was also visited by the *Llama* in search of furs, and in recognition of this an island in the sound near Olympia is now called McNeill's Island. The *Llama's* captain, incidentally, was one of the first to enter the harbor of Victoria—or, as it was then known, Camosun—noting that "in appearance the country for several miles was a natural beautiful park".[3]

Several stories are told of these early days. On one occasion, for example, it is said that on a northward journey along the B.C. coast a local Indian offered to pilot the *Llama* to a safe anchorage. At the place recommended by the native, the anchor was run out, but so deep was the water that the hawser snapped and the anchor was lost. Immediately, large numbers of canoes put out from the near-by shore in hopes that the inevitable shipwreck would provide rich plunder. McNeill, however, got his craft away successfully, though not before he had personally kicked the Indian overboard, there to search for what anchorage he might find.

McNeill's American citizenship was considered a difficulty, and for a time he was carried on the HBC books as a supercargo and trader, while James Allan Scarborough was officially listed as master.[4] It is not clear, indeed, whether McNeill ever acquired British citizenship; Douglas reported to his superiors in 1838 that McNeill was ready to do so "as soon as your Honors enable him to take the necessary steps",[5] but as late as 1843 he was still an American citizen.[6] Indeed, he had still not acquired British citizenship by 1852, for Douglas wrote to the secretary of the HBC in that year:

> I regret the difficulty that exists in regard to Captain McNeill's purchasing land and sincerely hope it may by some means be removed especially as Captain McNeill has been upwards of 17 years in the service of a British Company, soon after declared his intention of becoming a British subject and has been some time resident in this colony. I believe land has been acquired and held in Canada by persons who were not British subjects at the

Captain McNeill joins the Hudson's Bay Company

> time of purchase, and I hope that the Governor and Committee will use their influence in his behalf, as he has a large family born under the British flag, and will be exceedingly mortified should his application for land be rejected.[7]

So successful was McNeill in his early trading expeditions with the *Llama* that he soon incurred the hostility of the HBC, which understandably preferred the comfortable pleasures of monopoly to the uncertainties of competing with free enterprise.

In April 1832, the HBC ship *Cadboro*[8] attempted to drive the *Llama* from the southern Alaskan coast, but when the American trader showed its cannons, the *Cadboro* found it prudent to sail elsewhere.

A more effective method of eliminating competition was soon found by the Hudson's Bay Company; it decided to buy the *Llama* and to add McNeill to its list of employees. All parties were agreeable, and the ship was bought by Duncan Finlayson for the Company at a price of $5000, while McNeill became its employee at a salary of £200 per annum —£70 a year less, we might note, than he was receiving from the Boston owners. Finlayson evidently felt he had made a good bargain in both respects; in a letter to HBC headquarters, dated September 10, 1832, he noted that:

> The *Llama* was built six years since, & for three years of these she has cruised on the N.W. coast. She is coppered & copper fastened, perfectly sound in her plank timber, sails well, & is considered so very cheap, that I have since been offered seven thousand dollars for her.[9]

As to the *Llama's* captain, Finlayson gave it as his opinion that:

> The experience he has acquired of the natives & his intimate acquaintance with the different Harbors, Bays & Inlets of the Coast, from cruising thereon for the space of fifteen years—coupled with his activity talents & abilities as a Navigator & Trader—render him eminently qualified to give affairs in that quarter a favorable turn.[10]

In any event, McNeill was soon active for his new employers. In 1833 Captain Kipling of the brig *Dryad*[11] took material and stores from Fort Vancouver and Fort Nisqually to found Fort McLoughlin (situated near Bella Bella, and named after Chief Factor John McLoughlin). It was on this occasion that Llama Passage (on Fisher Channel in Fitzhugh Sound) received its name.

Various other services earned him the approval of the Company, and these, plus his detailed knowledge of the intricate coastline of the northwest coast,

The 'Beaver' as a working ship

As a hydrographic survey vessel, moored in Victoria Harbor, about 1862

Undergoing conversion on Cook's Way, Victoria, in the late 1870's

On freight and tug duty, about 1887. The man leaning against the nameboard is the mate; Capt. Marchant is standing just inside the wheelhouse door; David Symons, chief engineer, is in the middle of the group of three standing beside the smokestack; W. H. Evans, second engineer, is the farther of the pair at the rear of the upper deck housing; the Chinese cook is sitting on the after deck bulwark rail. Note the cattle on the after deck.

made him the natural choice for command of the *Beaver* in 1837. The steamer had passed the previous winter at Fort Simpson, and on the tenth of March, 1837 began the new season by sailing from there to Nass Harbor, 36 miles farther north, where it bought 70 furs from the natives. From there it touched at several places in search of furs, including Seal Harbor, Newittee, and two villages on Queen Charlotte Sound. After returning to Fort Simpson, the *Beaver* again set out for the ports previously visited, making every effort, in order that rival furtraders might be permanently discouraged, to gather all the furs available at those places; it was then dispatched to Fort Nisqually on Puget Sound.[12]

Even this voyage down the coast was put to good use, however, for Captain McNeill took the opportunity of making a careful examination of southern Vancouver Island, noting that he had found a good harbor, with land suited for farming near by, but lacking a river where mills could be established for making lumber and flour.

Douglas in a report to Governor George Simpson gave further details of McNeill's observations:

> On reaching the South end of the Island, a decided improvement was observed in the appearance of the Country. Three good harbours of easy access, were found west of Point Gonzalo, at two of which, Captain McNeill passed a few days. The land around these harbours is covered with wood to the extent of half a mile, interiorly, where the forest is replaced by a more open and beautifully diversified Country presenting a succession of plains with groves of oaks and pine trees, for a distance of 15 to 20 miles. The most Easterly of the harbours 10 miles West of Point Gonzalo is said to be the best on the Coast and possesses the important advantage, over the other, of a more abundant supply of fresh water, furnished by a stream 20 Yards wide, which after contributing to fertilize the open Country, flows into it. The plains are said to be fertile and covered with luxuriant vegetation; but judging from a sample of soil brought here, I think it rather light and certainly not the best quality, admitting even this disadvantage, I am persuaded that no part of this sterile & Rock bound coast will be found better adapted for the site of the proposed Depot or to combine, in a higher degree, the desired requisites, of a secure harbour accessible to shipping at every season, of good pasture, and to a certain extent, of improvable tillage land.[13]

As there had as yet been no definite decision to build a new trading post on southern Vancouver

The Beaver *earns its keep*

Island, this promising lead was not immediately followed up, but no doubt McNeill's observations were recalled when, a few years later, it became apparent that Fort Vancouver would soon be part of the United States, and that a new headquarters for the HBC on the Pacific Coast would have to be selected. Certainly the report of the *Beaver's* captain lingered in Douglas' mind, for in the fall of 1838, in a letter to the Governor and Committee in London, he referred to what would some day be the area of Victoria:

> The site examined by Captain McNeill, reported on in the 11th paragraph of my last letter, may not possess every advantage desirable, in such a situation, but it is, on the whole, decidedly unequalled by any other known portion of the coast north of the Columbia River.[14]

A few details of interest are available regarding the *Beaver's* first full year of operation on the Pacific coast. At the urging of Mr. Arthur, the chief engineer, it was laid up on one occasion for five weeks "under a course of alteration and repair"; moreover:

> . . . the vessel's rigging, which had always greatly retarded her progress, was altered, her heavy spars, a ponderous 9 pounder Gun, and all stores not wanted for immediate use laid up on shore; these changes having diminished her draught of water and consequent resistance she now travels at the hourly rate of 9 miles, being an improvement in speed of 1¼ mile p. hour.[15]

Altogether during 1837 the *Beaver* travelled a distance of 3504 miles, though the value of the furs it gathered had not much exceeded that taken by the sailing-ship *Llama;* Douglas reported that for 1835 the *Llama's* returns were £3667.10.6, that in 1836 the *Llama* was responsible for £3010.7.1 and the *Beaver* for £628.7.7, or a total of £3638.14.8, while in 1837 the *Beaver* had gathered £3734.8.1 worth of furs.[16] Douglas was, however, well satisfied with the Company's new acquisition.

For the next few years the *Beaver* performed useful tasks along the Pacific coast. Its log for the period from April 1837 to October 1841 is in the Provincial Archives, Victoria, and gives us an outline of its activities. Calling regularly at such ports as Fort Simpson, Seal Harbor, Newittee, Beaver Harbor, Fort Nass and McNeill Harbor, it secured from the natives a wide variety of furs—mink, raccoon, bear, marten, fisher, beaver, lynx and elk—and in return supplied the tribes with beads, axes,

Mutiny on the Beaver

knives, blankets, molasses, tobacco, combs, files, flints and vermilion.

One event in this period is not recorded in the log, which deals exclusively with goods bought and sold. This was a mutiny which broke out in January 1838, while the *Beaver* was laid up for the winter at Fort Simpson. According to a report later prepared by James Douglas for his superiors, McNeill beat two members of the crew with his cane for disobedience and abusive language. Later, two stokers received 24 lashes each for disobedience. The crew, stokers and engineers then refused to serve under McNeill. In crushing this rebellion, the officers "made several severe examples";[17] John Work then assumed command of the vessel temporarily and took it back to Fort Nisqually.

After investigating the affair, McLoughlin and Douglas decided that McNeill should be reinstated as captain. Four of the crew refused to sail under him, and were struck off the pay list, three of them later returning to England as crew members of the *Columbia*.[18]

Other less serious difficulties with members of the crew also occurred from time to time. The chief engineer, Peter Arthur, was in some respects unsatisfactory, Douglas reported to his superiors that:

> He is well qualified, and attentive to his duty; but his conduct in other respects has been improper, and his very intemperate habits detract considerably from his general merits.[19]

It has been asserted that in 1838 the *Beaver* visited California waters. An item in the Victoria *Colonist* for August 4, 1928 refers to an article in the *Peninsula Daily Herald* of Monterey, California, which had apparently been published shortly before. The article in the American newspaper is described as being by J. J. Shinabarger, and entitled, "The very first Pacific steamship." It is said to have been illustrated by a picture of the *Beaver* in Monterey Harbor. According to the *Colonist:*

> During 1838 the *Beaver* made a trip farther south than usual, aiming to land at Monterey for a cargo of hides, but by some error of navigation got into Carmel Bay instead. The Indians were terrified and fled to the hills at the sight of what they thought was some strange sea-monster. The priests at Carmel Mission entertained the ship's crew and directed them to Monterey.

However, the log of the *Beaver* for this period gives no suggestion of any such incident; more-

John McLoughlin visits southern Vancouver Island

over, Douglas in a letter to the Governor & Committee dated October 18, 1838 states that the *Beaver* in this year was "employed in her usual field of enterprise," and that "it is unnecessary to trace out the summer journeys of the *Beaver,* as they were confined to precisely the same harbours visited last year." It thus seems unlikely that there is any truth in this story of the *Beaver* having visited Californian waters.[20]

The *Beaver* was again actively collecting furs in 1839. Toward the end of the year, it carried McLoughlin to southern Vancouver Island, where he examined possible locations for a new post. He was not, however, satisfied with Camosun (later to be known as Victoria), reporting that "it is a very fine harbor accessible at all seasons, but is not a place suitable for our purpose."[21] McLoughlin's second-in-command, James Douglas, reported to London during this period concerning the *Beaver,* declaring:

> The steam vessel is in the highest order, her boilers are wearing, but the engine does not seem at all impaired by use, and works with the same ease and power as when first set in motion.[22]

Douglas recommended that Fort McLoughlin be retained, as:

> Steam vessels are exposed to many accidents, and should any misfortune prevent the *Beaver* from running, the consequences would be fatal to our interests.[23]

In 1840 the *Beaver* was assigned an important duty. This was to convey Douglas to Sitka, there to hold talks with the Russian authorities regarding matters connected with the fur trade. The *Beaver* was already, as we noted, showing signs of wear; the boilers were, however, patched up for the voyage and new ones ordered against the day when they would have to be replaced.

Douglas left Fort Vancouver on April 22, 1840, and almost immediately bad news was brought to him. A disastrous fire at Fort Langley had almost totally destroyed this important depot. In his diary he noted some details as reported to him:

> It broke out in the forge, consumed building after building with rapid and relentless fury, unquelled by the efforts made to arrest its course until the Fort lay a waste, reduced to a heap of smoking ruins. The trade goods, a bundle of furs, and seven barrels of salmon were alone rescued from the flames; houses, utensils, furniture, a large stock of salt provisions and all the seasoned barrel staves for the approaching fishery have fallen a sacrifice to the devouring element.[24]

James Douglas journeys to Alaska

Douglas was soon at the scene of the disaster, his entry for April 30 recording that:

> We left Fort Nisqually this morning at 6 o'clock in the steam vessel; anchored at dusk after a very smooth pleasant run in Strawberry Bay . . . and the following day reached Fort Langley at 4 o'clock in the afternoon.
>
> The work of destruction has been fearfully complete, extending to every part of the premises, of which a few blackened stumps alone remain.

Douglas and his men gave Chief Trader Yale,[25] in charge of the post, what help they could, and then on the fifth of May resumed their journey, anchoring at Feveda (Texada) Island, and then pushing on to the Comox area of Vancouver Island. On the eighth of May the *Beaver* anchored at McNeill's Harbor and the ship began trading with the natives, 20 sea otters and 70 beaver and land otters being obtained. Later Douglas proceeded to Newittee, Fort McLoughlin, Fort Simpson and Fort Stikine.

On the 25th of May he reached Sitka, where, in his own words, he "held daily conference with the Governor, in a frank and open manner, so as to dissipate all semblance of reserve and establish our intercourse on a basis of mutual confidence".[26] One interesting piece of information Douglas obtained from Governor Etholine was that the Russians were anxious to sell their post at Bodega Bay, near San Francisco, for $30,000. The 1500 sheep and 1000 horses and mules of this sizable outpost of the Russian company were also for sale, as well as numerous farm buildings. Governor Etholine also discussed with Douglas his need of blankets and butter and also (if the Bodega Bay farm changed hands) of beef.

After agreement had been reached on these and similar matters, the *Beaver* steamed away.[27] On the first of June, as had been agreed during the negotiations, Douglas' party took possession of Fort Stikine; the Union Jack was raised, and a salute of seven guns was fired.[28] Then the *Beaver* proceeded to Fort Simpson. Here the HBC ship *Vancouver* soon appeared and "we had her towed into harbour by the steam vessel."

On June 10, the *Beaver* left Fort Simpson, arriving the next day at Fort Stikine. Soon after leaving this latter place, Douglas' party was held up in Wrangell's Canal by an accident to the *Beaver;* no details, however, are given in Douglas' account.

In June a site was selected on the Taku River

Governor Simpson's account of his famous voyage

for a new fort (to be known as Fort Taku or Fort Durham).[29] By August it was completed, and Douglas, having garrisoned it, left in the *Beaver,* almost immediately discovering that the industrial revolution had also begun to affect the vast dominions of the Tsar; he "found the Russian steam vessel anchored in Barlow's Cove." More disquieting still was the discovery that the natives had sold all their available furs to it. Douglas advised them in future to take them to Fort Taku, and then set about exploring the channels and inlets of the area. Eventually, after touching at a number of ports and trading with the Indians, as well as cutting wood for the insatiable furnace of the *Beaver,* he arrived safe and sound on September 21 at Fort Langley.

By October 2 he was back at Fort Vancouver, where he found awaiting him a commission promoting him to the rank of Chief Factor.

The steamer was by this time showing signs of trouble; on Christmas Day, 1840, McNeill wrote to Simpson: "I am sorry to inform you that our boilers are getting the worse for wear; they are giving way fast and have been patched in many places . . ." Moreover, he went so far as to suggest that the *Beaver* should be either sold or converted to sail. Another suggestion was that a steamer of 600 tons be sent out, as the *Beaver* was too small to carry any sizable amount of cargo.[30]

On April 7, 1841 McNeill reported to Simpson that the steamer had twice broken down and would need extensive repairs.[31] McLoughlin, too, was dissatisfied with it, and on May 24 recommended to the Governor and Committee in London that it be converted to sail, which would, in his view, be in the long run more profitable for the Company. He noted that the boilers were in poor shape, and that the bottom of the flue had had to be patched, which, in Captain McNeill's words, was "the first time we have discovered any flaw in the bottom of the boilers or flues".[32]

Repairs were made and the steamer was ready by the late summer of 1841 for another important assignment. Sir George Simpson (as he had recently become) had decided on an extensive tour of the HBC empire. Setting out from London in March, he arrived in due course on the Pacific coast and was received at Fort Vancouver by James Douglas in the absence of John McLoughlin on August 25.

After a four day journey on horseback, Simpson reached Fort Nisqually, where he and Douglas went on board the *Beaver* and were soon headed northward. Simpson was later to write, or cause to have written, a detailed account of his journey around the globe in the service of the Company, and we are thus able to follow this portion of it in some detail. He recorded, for example:

> At noon on Monday went on board at Fort Nisqually. Starting under a salute of seven guns, we pushed along against a strong breeze, till we anchored about five in the afternoon to enable the engineer to repair some damage which the machinery had sustained; but the job being completed by nine, we then steamed on all night.
>
> About seven in the morning we passed along the inner end of Fuca's Straits, the first of the numberless inlets of this coast that was ever discovered by civilized man. The neighboring country, comprising the southern end of Vancouver's Island, is well adapted for cultivation; for, in addition to a tolerable soil and a moderate climate, it possesses excellent harbours and abundance of timber. It will doubtless become, in time, the most valuable section of the whole coast above California.
>
> As a foul wind and a heavy sea prevented us from making more than two miles and a half an hour, we resolved to wood and water behind Point Roberts, near the mouth of Fraser's River — a stream which, after traversing New Caledonia on its way from the Rocky Mountains, falls into the Gulf of Georgia in lat. 49° . . .
>
> Behind Point Roberts, there was a large camp of about a thousand savages, inhabitants of Vancouver's Island, who periodically cross the Gulf to Frazer's River, for the purpose of fishing. A great number of canoes assisted us in bringing our wood and water from the shore, some of them paddled entirely by young girls of remarkably interesting and comely appearance. These people offered us salmon, potatoes, berries and shell-fish for sale.
>
> The wind having moderated, we weighed anchor about one in the morning, and continued our course between Vancouver's Island and the mainland till three in the afternoon. The channel rarely exceeded six miles in width, and the shores on both sides were so mountainous, that the peaks, though situated only in 50° of latitude, were covered with perpetual snow. In the course of the forenoon, we crossed the parallel of the once famous Nootka Sound, breasting the open ocean on the other side of Vancouver's Island — an inlet which, after nearly involving Spain and England in war, was reduced into insignificance by the discovery of the very path which we were traversing.[33]

Later the *Beaver* anchored at Feveda (Texada)

Island, where it took on wood and water. Stops of this nature were a regular feature of voyages by the *Beaver,* and Simpson made some comments on this and related matters:

> We were detained the whole of the next day by the same indispensable business of supplying the steamer with fuel. In fact, as the vessel carries only one day's stock, about forty cords, and takes about the same time to cut the wood as to burn it, she is at least as much at anchor as she is under way; a good deal of her delay, however, being rendered necessary, without reference to the demands of her furnace, by wind and weather, and also for the purpose of dealing with the natives. Still, on the whole, the paddle is far preferable to canvas in these inland waters, which extend from Puget Sound to Cross Sound, by reason of the strength of the currents, the variableness of the winds, the narrowness of the channels, and the intricacy and ruggedness of the line of coast.[34]

In the vicinity of Comox, the steamer was surrounded by forty or fifty canoes full of natives. Their attitude was friendly, but they were not allowed on board, with one exception:

> We did allow a chief of the Quakeolths to embark, along with his wife and child; as he was desirous of obtaining a passage to his village, about seventy miles distant, while his canoe, a pretty little craft of about twelve paddles, was taken in tow. This was not this grandee's first trip in the *Beaver.* On a former occasion, he had made love to the captain's wife, who was accompanying her husband; and, when he found her obdurate, he transferred his attention to Mrs. Manson, who happened to be on board along with Mr. Manson himself, till, on being sent by her to negociate with her husband, he gravely backed his application by offering him a large bundle of furs. On the present occasion, also, this ardent admirer of the fair sex was true to his system, for he took a great fancy to an Englishwoman on board, while, at the same time, with more generosity than justice, he recommended his own princess, not to the woman's husband, but to myself.[35]

Eventually the *Beaver* reached McNeill's Harbor, where a lively trade with the Indians took place. Simpson gives us an interesting picture of the scene:

> The standard of prices being fixed after two hours of higgling, the business then went on briskly. To avoid the inconvenience and danger of a crowd, half a dozen only of the savages were to be admitted on deck at once; and, in order to enforce the regulation, five sentinels were stationed on the gangways, on the poop,

'Ullachan oil' and lip pieces

and on the paddle-boxes, while the boarding netting, as amounting to a mystery or a medicine, formed a better protection than all the watchmen put together.

Stationing himself at the steerage hatchway, Captain McNeill threw down each skin, as he examined it, with its price chalked on it—the equivalents being handed up from below by the two or three men that were in charge of the store.[36]

One interesting feature of these trading voyages was noted by Simpson with some amusement. Although boundless in admiration for McNeill, none of the natives could pronounce what seemed to them an incomprehensible appellation:

They made sad work, by the by, of his name; for, whenever his head showed itself above the bulwarks, young and old, male and female, vociferated, from every canoe, Ma-ta-hell, ma-ta-hell, ma-ta-hell—a word, which, with the comparative indistinctness of its first syllable, sounded very like a request on their part that the trader might go a great way beyond the engineer's furnace.[37]

The *Beaver* continued her voyage up the coast, stopping from time to time to trade with the natives. On at least one occasion, the ship demonstrated the superiority of steam over sail. Running into a thick fog, it attempted to return to harbor:

But we had hardly put about, when we heard the sound of breakers almost under our bow. "Stop her and back!" was passed to the engineer, and it was well that a word could do the needful, for a sailing vessel would have been knocked to pieces in less time than we took to return stern foremost into fifteen fathoms.[38]

Soon the *Beaver* was at Fort McLoughlin on Millbank Sound, where Charles Ross (one day to be in charge of Fort Victoria) was stationed. Several features of this distant part of the world engaged Simpson's attention; for example, a war-canoe of the "Ballabollas" (Bella Bella Indians):

It was sixty feet long, four and a half deep, and six and a half broad, with elevated prow and stern. This vessel would carry a hundred men, fifty engaged in paddling, and fifty stowed away; and yet, notwithstanding its enormous capacity, it was formed, with the exception of the raised portions of the extremities, out of a single log.[39]

Simpson was also attracted by "ullachan oil," his shrewd eye envisaging at once its commercial possibilities:

As this oil, by the way, was free from smell,

> it might be applied to many purposes in the civilized world, and I accordingly ordered a few jars of it to be sent to London by way of sample.[40]

Simpson was not, however, much taken by "that disgusting ornament of the fair sex, the lip-piece."

Eventually the *Beaver* reached Fort Stikine, recently leased from Russia for ten years, and then went on to Fort Taku. Finally, it steamed into Sitka, where Douglas and Simpson went ashore to pay their respects to the Russian governor Etholine. Simpson soon found he had one thing, at least, in common with the Governor's wife: as he was now at the farthest extremity of the globe from London, so she had arrived at this remote spot from Finland. The guests received "a good dinner in the French style," and Simpson held useful business conversations with the Governor. One of the most important results of these was that the two great fur companies decided on economic policies which would have the effect of dividing the fur trade between them, and excluding American competition by making it unprofitable for independent traders.

Before long, the *Beaver* was making its way southward again. At a locality in the northern part of Vancouver Island, the natives asked the whites to erect a trading-post. This, however, was contrary to Simpson's policy, as:

> The mysterious steamer, against which neither calms nor contrary winds were any security, possessed, in our estimation, this advantage over stationary forts, that, besides being as convenient for the purposes of trade, she was the terror, whether present or absent, of every tribe on the coast.[41]

Simpson was, indeed, highly pleased with the little steamer, noting that:

> This labryinth of waters is peculiarly adapted for the powers of steam. In the case of a sailing vessel, our delays and dangers would have been tripled and quadrupled—a circumstance which raised my estimate of Vancouver's skill and perseverance every step of my progress. But, independently of physical advantages, steam, as I have already mentioned, may be said to exert an almost superstitious influence over the savages; besides acting without intermission on their fears, it has, in a great measure, subdued their very love of robbery and violence. In a word, it has inspired the red man with a new opinion—new not in degree but in kind—of the superiority of his white brother.[42]

Eventually Simpson's party reached Puget Sound once more. An interesting anecdote confirming

McLoughlin and Simpson disagree

Simpson's judgment as to the psychological value of the *Beaver* is given at this point in his narrative:

> After the arrival of the emigrants from Red River, their guide, a Cree of the name of Bras Croche, took a short trip in the *Beaver*. When asked what he thought of her — "Don't ask me," was his reply: "I cannot speak; my friends will say that I tell lies when I let them know what I have seen; Indians are fools and know nothing; I can see that the iron machinery makes the ship to go, but I cannot see what makes the iron machinery itself to go." Bras Croche, though very intelligent, and, like all the Crees, partially civilized, was nevertheless so full of doubt and wonder that he would not leave the vessel till he got a certificate to the effect that he had been on board of a ship which needed neither sails nor paddlers. Though not one of his countrymen would understand a word of what was written, yet the most skeptical among them would not dare to question the truth of a story which had a document in its favour.[43]

From Fort Vancouver, Simpson descended the Columbia to Fort George (Astoria) at its mouth, where he took passage for San Francisco and later for Honolulu. From there, we might note, he once again visited Fort Stikine and Sitka, and then proceeded homeward across the entire width of the Russian Empire.

Simpson had travelled, as always, at lightning speed, but this had not prevented him from reaching some highly important decisions, which he would soon have enforced over the protests of his reluctant subordinate McLoughlin. These were to close Forts McLoughlin, Stikine and Taku, and to retain only Fort Simpson as a northern supply depot. The place in the fur trade of the abandoned posts would be taken by the *Beaver*. Simpson also now gave more active consideration to the transfer of HBC headquarters on the Pacific coast from Fort Vancouver to some location, not yet determined, on Puget Sound[44] or Vancouver Island, a step made desirable by the dangerous bar off the mouth of the Columbia and the likelihood that the boundary between British and American possessions in the northwest would be drawn considerably north of that river.

Late in 1841, Simpson communicated these decisions, or rather recommendations, to his superiors in London. He estimated that the *Beaver* could call about six times a season at the important Indian settlements along the coast, calculated that the revenues of the Company would soon be expanding under the projected new policy, and suggested that another steamer should be added to the HBC fleet in case of a serious accident to the *Beaver*.[45]

McLoughlin, however, was still unconvinced as to the wisdom of Simpson's new policy, and a conference between the two men was held at Honolulu in February 1842.[46] McLoughlin had come provided with statistics to prove that the *Beaver* had lost money in every season since it arrived on the Pacific coast,[47] but Simpson was immovable. McLoughlin was ordered to abandon Forts McLoughlin and Taku (and Fort Stikine at a slightly later date), and to build a new depot on southern Vancouver Island. The site of the latter was to be determined after a careful survey of possible locations, Simpson noting that it must be one . . .

> combining, if possible, all the advantages required, the most important of which are a safe and accessible harbour, well situated for defence, with water-power for Grist and Saw Mills, abundance of timber for Home Consumption and Exportation, and the adjacent country well adapted for tillage and pasture farms on an extensive scale.[48]

Simpson also ordered McLoughlin to have constructed "a decked lighter, of about 150 tons," which the *Beaver* would tow, explaining that:

> This lighter should be considered as part and parcel of the vessel, to accompany her everywhere, which she can do without any material hindrance or inconvenience, from Puget Sound up to Cross Sound, the whole of that inland navigation being adapted, as if specially by nature, for such mode of transport.[49]

McLoughlin had no choice but to obey, though he continued for some time to lodge protests and warnings of disaster with both Simpson and the supreme authorities of the Company in London. For example, on June 24, 1842 he informed the Governor and Committee that it was painful "to see large sums of money lost to no purpose",[50] while in October, in another letter to them, he stoutly maintained that "the advantages of the Establishments over the steamer are so self-evident that I cannot see how a person possessed of the least knowledge of the business can maintain a different opinion".[51] In November he submitted figures purporting to prove that whereas in 1835 the *Llama* had traded £3667. 10. 6 worth of furs and yielded a profit of £1196. 13. 3, in 1837 the *Beaver* had traded £3741. 3. 1 worth of furs and lost £960. 8. 0.[52]

Wear and tear

Simpson, however, was viewing the question in a wider perspective than McLoughlin;[53] their differing points of view were ably reflected and summed up in a letter written in this period to Simpson by Alexander Anderson, an old-time employee of the Company in the northwest, who was later to have a prominent part in finding a route for the fur brigades from central British Columbia to the lower Fraser River:

> It is, I know, become quite general to decry the merits of that valuable craft and her utility in the past transactions on the coast, but with deference to the judgment of others my own partial experience induces me to conclude that it is to the steamer chiefly that we are indebted for the recent absence of competition in that direction and which the politic arrangement since concluded for supplying the Russian colony with merchandise will tend to perpetuate. Energetic measures alone could have suppressed an evil which a vacillating policy must only have fostered and encouraged. In such a case it is unfair to estimate the claims of a measure by the narrow rules of immediate pecuniary profit; it is necessary to adopt a more expanded view of the question and to contemplate the probability of ulterior advantage notwithstanding actual preliminary loss may be incurred. But I fear the former has been too much the case with the *Beaver* and that reference has been more frequently had to the state of her account current in the Fort Vancouver ledger than to the wider field of investigation she was justly entitled to demand.[54]

Not everything, however, had gone perfectly with the little steamer. In the summer of 1842 it was discovered that seventeen planks were rotten on the starboard side of the forecastle and would have to be replaced,[55] while Mr. Carless the engineer[56] informed McNeill that the boilers were in such poor condition that the steamer would have to be laid up until new ones were installed.[57] McLoughlin was obliged to apologize to Governor Etholine for not shipping a quantity of pelts (promised to the Russian American Company in return for British rights in the Alaskan Panhandle granted by the Russians under the agreement of 1839) from Fort Simpson to Sitka, due to "the unfortunate state of the boilers".[58]

The new boilers eventually arrived and were installed. The *Beaver* was now ready for any new assignment, and the year 1843 was to see a highly important one. This was the establishment of the new depot on southern Vancouver Island, intended to become the eventual headquarters of the HBC on

Douglas investigates the harbors of southern Vancouver Island

the Pacific coast. The previous summer, Douglas, using the *Cadboro,* had made a detailed examination of possible locations for the new establishment. The advantages and disadvantages of those harbors now known as Sooke, Metchosin, Esquimalt and Victoria were closely estimated, with Douglas giving it as his own view that the last of these was the most suitable for the purposes of the Company. He noted that:

> At Camosack there is a pleasant and convenient Site for the Establishment within Fifty Yards of the Anchorage, on the Border of a large Tract of clear Land, which extends eastward to Point Gonzalo at the south-east extremity of the Island and about Six Miles interiorly being the most picturesque and decidedly the most valuable Part of the Island that we had the good Fortune to discover . . .
>
> As a harbour it is equally safe and accessible and abundance of timber grows on it for home consumption and exportation. There being no fresh water stream of sufficient power, flour or saw mills may be erected in the Canal of Camosack at a Point where the Channel is constricted to the breadth of forty-seven feet by two Ridges of Granite projecting from either bank into the Canal, through which the Tide rushes out and in with a degree of Force and Velocity capable of driving the most powerful Machinery, if guided and applied by mechanical Skill.[59]

The higher authorities of the Company agreed with Douglas as to the best location for the new establishment, and accordingly he set out in the spring of 1843 to initiate the new venture. As in 1841, the *Beaver* was ready just in time to take its part in the making of history, and its anchor was dropped about four in the afternoon of March 14 somewhere in the vicinity of Shoal Bay (more correctly known as McNeill Bay) and Clover Point.

One unusual feature of this famous event is that it is not known for certain who was the captain of the *Beaver* on this historic occasion. It has often been asserted that it was W. H. McNeill; this, however, is impossible, as Capt. McNeill was in England in the fall of 1842, and from there made a visit to his relatives in Boston in the summer of 1843. He then returned to England and in August of that year brought the *Cowlitz* back to Fort Vancouver.[60]

The man in charge of the *Beaver* when Douglas founded Fort Victoria was almost certainly one of two men: William Brotchie or Alexander Duncan. The former commanded the steamer from some time

The founding of Fort Victoria, 1843

in 1842 till some time in 1843, and the latter from some time in 1843 until November 1844, but the exact moment of transfer of command seems impossible to determine.

Brotchie, born in Caithness, Scotland in 1799, had served the HBC for a considerable period. He had been on the brig *Dryad* in 1831; later he had commanded the *Cadboro* from 1835 to 1838 and the *Nereide* in 1839. He was also the first captain of the *Cowlitz*, which had been built in 1840 for the Company and first arrived at Fort Vancouver on March 6, 1841.

About Alexander Duncan rather less is known. He had, however, commanded the *Dryad* in 1834.[61]

As to which of these two men brought Douglas to Victoria that March day in 1843, it is not yet possible to speak with certainty.[62] It would seem that in this period captains were often assigned to such ships as at any given moment might seem best to their superiors, a practice which though probably useful to the Company is vexing to the historian. There is enough evidence, however, in the volumes of Company history thus far published by the Hudson's Bay Record Society to narrow the final choice fairly conclusively to these two men, but beyond this it is not yet possible to go.[63]

At all events, on March 15 Douglas and his party went ashore and soon men were at work digging a well, making timber or engaging the local Indians to do so, and erecting a few buildings and a stockade.[64]

Once the work was well under way, Douglas left in the *Beaver* to pick up the men and supplies of Forts Durham (Taku) and McLoughlin, which were now to be abandoned. Early in June he was back, and with these reinforcements the work went ahead more rapidly. Charles Ross was put in charge, with Roderick Finlayson as his assistant, while Douglas returned to Fort Vancouver and the *Beaver* to its base in Puget Sound.

And so it was that once again the serviceable little craft had aided in opening up the northwest and binding together its small and scattered settlements. Moreover, it had now played its part in founding the future capital city of Canada's most westerly province. Admittedly, it had done so on behalf of a commercial enterprise, but at the same time the indispensable foundation was being laid for enduring political units—the colonies of Vancouver Island and later British Columbia, and, looming up dimly behind them, the future Dominion of Canada. If the empire of fur had not expanded and prospered, the political empire which succeeded and absorbed it might never have come into being; as a modest contributor to this great evolving process, the *Beaver* had already deserved well of those who would inhabit the Pacific coast in days to come.

Footnotes

[1] McLoughlin to Governor & Committee, Nov. 15, 1836. *The Letters of John McLoughlin,* first series, 1825-1838, ed. E. E. Rich, Toronto, the Champlain Society, 1941, p. 152.

Captain Home was drowned on February 12, 1838, while attempting to cross the Columbia River in a small sailboat. Home Bay, Princess Royal Island, Whale Channel is named after him. See Walbran, *British Columbia Coast Names,* Ottawa, 1909, pp. 244-5.

[2] The authoritative *Letters of John McLoughlin* (third series, the Champlain Society, Toronto, 1944, p. 314) gives the date as 1801, but McNeill himself, in a legal declaration made Sept. 27, 1871 before M. W. Tyrwhitt Drake, Notary Public, declared, "I am 68 years of age, and at 20 years of age I became a master mariner."

An article in the Victoria *Colonist* for July 18, 1920, based on material supplied by McNeill's grandson, then keeper of the Fiddle Reef light-house off Oak Bay, Victoria, states that he was born in Edinburgh. This seems quite unlikely, in view of the references elsewhere to the difficulties occasioned by his American citizenship. We might note, though, that Douglas, in a letter dated Oct. 18, 1838 to the London headquarters of the HBC, speaks of McNeill having agreed to "return to the country and allegiance of his forefathers." (*Letters of John McLoughlin,* first series, p. 237.)

McNeill evidently felt divided loyalties at times. In 1869, when a petition was presented to President Grant, supporting the annexation of British Columbia to the United States, the Captain, then retired, was one of the signatories (*Letters of John McLoughlin,* third series, p. 318; see also W. E. Ireland, "The Annexation Petition of 1869" in *BCHQ,* Vol. IV, No. 4, October 1940.)

[3] *Colonist,* July 18, 1920. An article in the *Colonist* for April 12, 1925 states that the *Llama* was the first ship

to anchor in Victoria harbor and the *Cadboro* under Captain Scarborough the second.

At some point during this period, McNeill married Matilda, daughter of an Indian chief. Dr. Helmcken in his "Reminiscences" describes her as "a very large handsome Kijani woman, with all the dignity and carriage of a chieftainess, which she was." (The Kijani are a division of the Haida language-group.)

The McNeills had three sons and six daughters before Matilda died in 1850 following the birth of twins. These nine children were:

1. William. He became the master of a mail and passenger boat which plied between Fort Nisqually and Victoria. He also helped explore the Queen Charlotte Islands, and urged the erection of a light-house on Trial Island, Oak Bay. On June 3, 1853 he married Mary, the daughter of Donald Macaulay, who had served with McNeill on the *Llama,* and who was accidentally drowned in Esquimalt Harbor in 1868 (*Colonist,* Sept. 21, 1868). At the time of his death he was in charge of the Company's powder magazine in Esquimalt; Macaulay Point is named after him. William McNeill died October 29, 1889 in his 57th year (*Colonist,* Oct. 31, 1889). His son, Donald Henry McNeill, born June 27, 1854, became an explorer and prospector for the government, and helped to promote the settlement of the Comox Valley and to fix the boundary between Alaska and the North West Territories. In 1894 he called the first public meeting to consider a public school for Oak Bay, and later served as a school trustee for seven years. In charge of the Fiddle Reef light-house, Oak Bay, from March 1905 to January 1925 (*Colonist,* April 12, 1925), he died on January 13, 1928 (see *Colonist* and *Times* for January 14, 1928).

2. Harry.

3. Alfred. Information concerning these two sons is very scanty. The *Colonist* for May 6, 1882, however, in reporting a complex case then before the B.C. Supreme Court regarding Capt. McNeill's will, noted that Alfred was living abroad.

4. Helen. In July 1846 she married George Blenkinsop (born 1822), described by Dr. Helmcken as "a courageous, good-natured, active, intelligent Cornishman" and by Sir George Simpson as "one Blenkinsop, who, though merely a common sailor, was of regular habits and possessed a good education" (*Narrative of a journey round the world during the years 1841 and 1842,* London, 1847, Vol., 2, p. 183.) He served the HBC at Fort Stikine and also under Capt. W. H. McNeill at Fort Rupert in 1850 while Richard Blanshard was Governor of Vancouver Island (see my *Victoria: The Fort.* Mitchell Press, Vancouver, 1968. p. 87). Later he was employed in the bakery at Craigflower Farm, and still later helped to survey the route for the CPR. The Blenkinsops had seven children: Charles Henry, who died March 2, 1864 at the age of 16 (*Colonist,* March 5, 1864); Robert, who went down in the steamship *Teuton* off South Africa at the age of 31 (*Colonist,* Oct. 11, 1881, p. 3); John George and William Henry, both baptized on January 25, 1858; Mary Denny (commonly called Fanny), baptized April 30, 1860, who was married by Bishop Cridge on Oct. 10, 1885 to John Hicks; Frederick William, baptized August 1865; Francis Drummond, baptized Dec. 29, 1867. Mrs. Blenkinsop died March 26, 1869 at the age of 40 (*Colonist,* March 27, 1869), and her husband later married a girl from Fort Rupert at Alert Bay, known as "Miss Emma" (*Colonist,* Aug. 17, 1884).

5. Lucy, who married Hamilton Moffat on March 15, 1856. Moffatt, born at Shanklin, Isle of Wight, came to B.C. in the *Cowlitz* in 1850. He worked for the HBC for 22 years, becoming a Chief Trader. He died at

Victoria April 13, 1894, at the age of 62, leaving his widow but no children (*Colonist,* April 14, 1894).

6. Matilda, who on January 18, 1861 was married to Robert Jesse at Pendennis Farm, Cedar Hill by the Rev. Cridge (*Colonist,* Jan. 25, 1861). A son was born to her on Jan. 4, 1877 (*Colonist,* Jan. 5, 1877); another, Robert, in 1879, and a third, Herbert, on Sept. 30, 1881 at Tunnel City (15-mile camp), near Yale (*Colonist,* Oct. 9, 1881). The *Colonist* for Dec. 21, 1882 reported the recent death of their father from dropsy. Robert Jesse, junior, was at one time manager of the Brackman-Ker feed store in Victoria, retiring in 1939; he died May 5, 1950 (*Colonist,* May 6, 1950). Herbert Jesse died a few weeks later on June 6, 1950 (*Colonist,* June 9, 1950).

7. Fanny, who married Judson Young on August 1, 1864. In November, 1872 he was one of the pall-bearers at the funeral of Capt. John Swanson, one-time Captain of the *Beaver.*

8. Rebecca (one of the twins); she was married by Bishop Cridge on Oct. 4, 1879 to Thomas Elwyn, eldest son of Lt-General Elwyn (*Colonist,* Oct. 5, 1879). On Jan. 31, 1891, the *Colonist* reported that "Mr. J. A. Baker, eldest son of the late Major Alfred Baker, Bengal Civil Service, was on Monday (Jan. 26) married to the widow of the late Mr. Thomas Elwyn of Victoria. The marriage took place in the Episcopal Church at Kamloops, Rev. A. Shildrick officiating."

9. Harriet (the other twin) married John Jane on October 9, 1889 at Savona's Ferry (*Colonist,* Oct. 15, 1889) and later John David Jones. The latter died at the age of 84 on Feb. 21, 1934 (Victoria *Daily Times,* Feb. 22, 1934).

Captain McNeill married a second time, but the records of this marriage have never been found, and its date is not known. His wife's name was Martha, and she was an Indian, probably of the Nass tribe. She was apparently illiterate, as her will is signed with a mark. She died in October 1883 (*Colonist,* Oct. 6, 1883). There were no children of this marriage.

[4] See *Letters of John McLoughlin, third series,* p. 316. Herbert George Scarborough had been second mate of the *Isabella,* lost on the Columbia bar in May 1830. He later became first mate of the *Llama* and *Beaver,* and master of the *Cadboro* and *Mary Dare.* He married Ann Elizabeth, a Chinook Indian, at Fort Vancouver on October 30, 1843, and died on February 4, 1855. Douglas described him as "a quiet inoffensive man, a good sailor and careful steady officer." (Douglas to Governor & Committee, Oct. 14, 1839, *Letters of John McLoughlin, second series,* p. 208).

When McNeill brought the *Cowlitz* to the Pacific coast in 1843, William Heath was listed as its nominal commander (*Letters of John McLoughlin, third series,* p. 317).

[5] Douglas to Governor & Committee, October 18, 1838. *Letters of John McLoughlin, first series,* p. 237.

[6] *Letters of John McLoughlin, third series,* p. 317.

[7] Douglas to Barclay, June 23, 1852. PABC.

[8] The *Cadboro* (56 feet long, 72 tons, 6 guns) was built at Rye, Sussex in 1824, sailed from London in the fall of 1826 and arrived at Fort Vancouver in the spring of 1827 under the command of Captain Swan. Lieutenant Simpson of the Royal Navy then took command of her until 1831. She was later commanded by Captain Sinclair from 1831 to 1833, by Captain William Ryan from 1833 to 1835, and by Captain Brotchie (after whom Brotchie's Ledge, off Victoria, is named) from 1835 to 1838. Captain James Scarborough was in charge of her from 1838 to 1848, and James Sangster from 1848 to 1854. In 1860 the HBC sold the *Cadboro* at auction for

$2450, and it was used as a coal and lumber vessel in the Victoria area until October 1862, when it was lost in a gale near Port Angeles (*Colonist*, Oct. 8, 1862). Cadboro Bay was named after the schooner by HBC officials about 1842 (Walbran, *British Columbia Coast Names*, p. 66). See also Lewis and Dryden's *Marine History of the Pacific Northwest*, ed. E. W. Wright, Antiquarian Press, New York, 1961, p. 13 and W. F. Tolmie's diary, published under the title *Physician and Fur Trader* by Mitchell Press, Vancouver in 1963, p. 29.

[9] Finlayson to William Smith (secretary of the HBC), *Letters of John McLoughlin, first series,* p. 336.

[10] *Ibid.*, p. 337. It is interesting to note that Finlayson implies that McNeill had been sailing on the northwest coast as early as 1817.

[11] The *Dryad* had arrived on the Pacific coast in 1831. In 1834 it became the focus of an international incident. When sent to build a fur-trading post for the HBC on the Stikine River, it was refused permission to do so by the commander of the Russian ship *Chichagoff,* who rejoiced in the name of Dionysius Zarembo. The British government was induced to lodge a protest with the Russian government, claiming that the Russian action was a violation of an agreement reached in 1825 which gave British ships the right to trade in certain Russian coastal waters for a period of ten years. The HBC used the diplomatic advantage derived from this incident to persuade the Russian company to enter into an agreement in 1839 for dividing the fur trade between them, and excluding independent American traders from the north Pacific coast. See J. S. Galbraith, *The Hudson's Bay Company as an Imperial Factor 1821-1869,* U. of Toronto Press, 1957, pp. 146-155.

Another HBC vessel on the northwest coast in this period was the *Ganymede* (213 tons) which replaced the *William and Ann,* wrecked on the Columbia bar in 1829. Built at Chepstow in 1827, it sailed from Plymouth for the Columbia on September 16, 1828. It was on the Pacific coast 1832-34, in the region of Hudson's Bay in 1834, and on the Pacific coast again from 1834 to 1837. It was then returned to London where it was sold for £1700. The *Ganymede* was the ship which brought Dr. W. F. Tolmie (1812-1886) to the Pacific northwest. See Lewis and Dryden's *Marine History of the Pacific Northwest,* p. 14, and also Dr. Tolmie's Diary, published under the title *Physician and Fur Trader,* Mitchell Press, Vancouver, 1963, pp. 1-7.

[12] Fort Nisqually was the main station of the Puget Sound Agricultural Company, a subsidiary of the HBC. It produced large quantities of farm products for Company posts and also for export to the Russian establishment at Sitka.

There are interesting articles on Fort Nisqually in the HBC magazine *Beaver* for September 1934 and September 1940.

[13] Douglas to Simpson, March 18, 1838. *The Letters of John McLoughlin, first series,* p. 287.
Point Gonzalo is now called Ten Mile Point.

[14] Douglas to Governor & Committee, October 18, 1838. *Letters of John McLoughlin, first series,* p. 267.

[15] Douglas to Simpson, March 18, 1838. *Letters of John McLoughlin, first series,* p. 273.

[16] These details are taken from a letter from Douglas to Simpson dated March 18, 1838. *Letters of John McLoughlin, first series,* p. 273.

[17] Douglas to Governor & Committee, October 18, 1838. *Letters of John McLoughlin,* first series, p. 246.

[18] *Letters of John McLoughlin,* second series, p. 21.
McLoughlin in a letter to the Governor & Committee on October 31, 1842, speaks of "a mutiny on board the

steamer when Capt. Home commanded her" (*Letters of John McLoughlin,* second series, p. 80), but I think this is a slip of the pen, and that he had this mutiny in mind.

The archivist of the Hudson's Bay Company, in response to an enquiry, has supplied the following additional information: "We have at present no information regarding any mutiny aboard the *Beaver* while she was under the command of Captain Home. A mutiny occurred on the *Nereide* (Captain Home) about the end of May 1837, and as you know McNeill was in command of the *Beaver* during the January 1838 mutiny. If McLoughlin is referring to either of these mutinies, his copyist has made an error."

[19] Douglas to Governor & Committee, Oct. 18, 1838. *Letters of John McLoughlin,* first series, p. 248. Liquor would seem to have been a problem on the *Beaver.* On Feb. 23, 1845 Capt. McNeill wrote to Simpson: "Lattie is on shore at Fort Simpson, turned out of the steamer for habitual drunkenness." (*Letters of John McLoughlin,* second series, p. xiii.) Lattie was discharged by Captain Charles Humphreys early in 1842 (*Ibid.,* p. 141). Captain Humphreys, appointed to the command of the *Beaver* in November 1844, when later questioned himself by his superiors about his drinking habits, admitted "having been twice intoxicated since a Master Mariner in the Hon. Co's service, on both occasions after a safe arrival at Woahoo." (*Ibid.,* p. 392. "Woahoo" is not an attempt by Capt. Humphreys to recapture his feelings on these occasions, but a reference to Oahu in the Hawaiian Islands.) The last captain of the *Beaver,* George Marchant, was also no stranger to the bottle.

[20] Douglas to Governor & Committee, *Letters of John McLoughlin,* first series, p. 247.

Capt. Brotchie, at one time captain of the *Beaver,* took the *Nereide* to Monterey in May 1838 to purchase sheep, and this may be the explanation of this story (*Letters of John McLoughlin,* third series, p. xxi).

[21] McLoughlin to Simpson, March 20, 1840. *Letters of John McLoughlin,* second series, p. 231.

[22] Douglas to Governor & Committee, October 14, 1839. *Letters of John McLoughlin,* second series, p. 215.

[23] *Ibid.,* p. 214.

[24] Diary of a trip to the northwest coast, April 22 — October 2, 1840. Unpublished MS in PABC.

[25] James Murray Yale was born in 1800. He entered the service of the HBC about 1815. He was stationed at Fort Langley soon after it was founded in 1827 and remained there till his retirement from the Company in 1860, becoming a Chief Factor in 1844, and being in charge of the Fort when the new colony of British Columbia was proclaimed there by James Douglas (appointed its first governor) on November 19, 1858. He died in 1871 at the age of 71 at his home "Stromness" on Burnside Road, Victoria; his grave is in the Quadra Street Cemetery, Pioneer Square.

[26] One important subject of discussion was an agreement concluded in February 1839 between the two great fur companies. This provided for the leasing for ten years by the British company of a narrow strip of Russian territory between the Portland Canal and Mount Fairweather; in return the HBC was to supply the Russians with a fixed number of furs each year, and also with agricultural products from its farms in the Puget Sound area. For a detailed account of this subject see two articles in the *BCHQ* for January 1941: D. C. Davidson's "Relations of the Hudson's Bay Company with the Russian American Company on the Northwest Coast, 1829-1867" and Willard Ireland's "James Douglas and the Russian American Company." Also Galbraith, *The*

Hudson's Bay Company as an Imperial Factor, 1821-1869, U. of Toronto Press, 1957, p. 154.

[27] For Douglas' perceptive comments on Russian business practices and organization, see my *James Douglas: Servant of Two Empires* (Mitchell Press, Vancouver, 1969), Chapter 3.

[28] W. G. Rae was placed in charge of this new HBC post, with John McLoughlin, junior, as his assistant. Young McLoughlin was later to have a tragic end, which further deepened the growing estrangement between his father and Simpson. See *Letters of John McLoughlin,* second series, pp. xxii-xliv.

[29] Dr. Kennedy was placed in charge, with Roderick Finlayson as his assistant. Finlayson, born in Ross-shire in 1818, joined the HBC about 1837. In 1841 he was transferred to Fort Stikine and later to Fort Simpson. In the spring of 1843 he landed with Douglas to found Fort Victoria, being placed in charge of this new post upon the death of Charles Ross in 1844. When Douglas assumed control of the post in 1849, Finlayson became Chief Accountant, and on December 14 of that year married Sarah, daughter of John Work, by whom he had seven daughters and four sons. He was made a Chief Trader in 1850, a Chief Factor in 1859, and retired from the HBC in 1872. He was mayor of Victoria in 1878, and died on January 20, 1892. Finlayson Channel and Roderick Island in it are named after him (Walbran, *British Columbia Coast Names,* p. 427). Finlayson Island is named after Duncan Finlayson, the uncle of Roderick Finlayson. Sarah Point on it, and Sarah Island in Finlayson Entrance, Millbank Sound, are named after Roderick Finlayson's wife, who died on Jan. 25, 1906 (Walbran, *Op. Cit.,* p. 179). Finlayson Channel was given its name by Capt. Charles Dodd around 1845, and the names of the other localities were chosen by Capt. Pender while in command of the *Beaver* during its period as a survey ship, probably in 1866 or 1867.

[30] McNeill to Simpson, Dec. 25, 1840. *Letters of John McLoughlin,* second series, p. xiv.

[31] *Loc. cit.*

[32] See McLoughlin to Governor and Committee, May 24, 1841. *Ibid.,* p. 36.

[33] Simpson, *Narrative of a journey round the world during the years 1841 and 1842,* London, 1847, pp. 181-183.

[34] *Ibid.,* p. 185

[35] *Ibid.,* pp. 186-7.

[36] *Ibid.,* p. 188.

[37] *Ibid.,* pp. 192-3.
McNeill's reputation among the Indians may be judged from the fact that he is one of the few white men to appear on a totem pole. Eric Sismey in an article in the *Colonist* for April 10, 1960 describes his discovery at the deserted Indian village of Hkusan of this interesting relic, noting how "to my surprise the figure at the top of the pole was that of a white man dressed in a buttoned tunic, ornamented with piping. The feet were well apart and the hands were deep in the slash pockets of seamen's trousers." Sismey's subsequent investigations leave no doubt that this figure represented McNeill (see also *Colonist* for June 17, 1962).

[38] Simpson, *Op. cit.,* p. 200.

[39] *Ibid.,* p. 204.

[40] *Ibid.,* p. 206.

[41] *Ibid.,* p. 236.

[42] *Ibid.,* p. 241.

[43] *Ibid.,* pp. 241-2.

[44] Puget Sound was named after Peter Puget, second lieutenant of Captain George Vancouver's ship *Discovery* (Walbran, *British Columbia Coast Names,* p. 404).

[45] Simpson to Governor & Committee, Nov. 25, 1841. *Letters of John McLoughlin,* second series, p. xvi.

[46] The HBC had an agency in Hawaii for a time, but withdrew from the islands in 1859. An interesting article in the *Beaver* for Sept. 1941 notes that a building in Hawaii still had a weathervane embodying a metal beaver, perhaps the last relic of the island's connection with the HBC.

[47] *Letters of John McLoughlin,* second series, p. xix.

[48] Simpson to McLoughlin, March 1, 1842. *Letters of John McLoughlin,* second series, p. 262.

[49] *Ibid.,* p. 264.

[50] *Ibid.,* p. 58.

[51] McLoughlin to Governor & Committee, Oct. 31, 1842. *Letters of John McLoughlin,* second series, p. 71.

[52] McLoughlin to Governor & Committee, Nov. 4, 1842. *Letters of John McLoughlin,* second series, p. 102.

[53] Simpson had the rare ability to combine the planning of grand strategy with attention to the most minute details. For example, on May 18, 1842 he wrote to McLoughlin:

"Scarborough I understand took his family to sea on board the *Cadboro* last year without permission. This is highly irregular & improper & I have to beg that a charge be made against him on account for their board, according to the scale determined upon last winter, & that positive orders be issued that no families nor passengers of any description be taken on board any ship without especial authority from you." (*Ibid.,* p. 294.)

[54] J. R. Anderson, Notes and Comments (unpublished manuscript in Provincial Archives, Victoria), pp. 43-44.

[55] McLoughlin to Governor & Committee, June 24, 1842. *Letters of John McLoughlin,* second series, p. 58.

[56] Joseph Carless had worked for six years for Boulton and Watt. In a contract signed Dec. 5, 1839 he agreed to serve the HBC as an engineer for five years at £150 per annum plus maintenance for himself and family. He and his wife Maria sailed from London in the *Forager* in January 1840 and arrived at Fort Vancouver in September, then proceeding to Nisqually. Simpson raised his salary to £176 per annum as from June 1, 1841. On the expiry of his contract, as no suitable replacement was available, he stayed on for an extra year at £250 per annum. On Dec. 12, 1846 he and his wife and their two children (born in the Oregon Territory) sailed in the *Vancouver* from Fort Victoria, arriving safely in London in July 1847. (See *Letters of John McLoughlin,* second series, p. 388.)

[57] McLoughlin to Governor & Committee, June 24 and Oct. 31, 1842. *Letters of John McLoughlin,* second series, pp. 58 and 71.

[58] McLoughlin to Etholine, May 16, 1842. *Letters of John McLoughlin,* second series, p. 326.

[59] The "Canal of Camosack" is now known as "the Gorge." The full text of Douglas' report to McLoughlin, dated July 12, 1842, is in the *Beaver* for March 1943.

[60] As he was still not a British subject, William Heath was listed as the nominal commander for this voyage. (*Letters of John McLoughlin,* third series, pp. 316-317.)

[61] See Walbran, *British Columbia Coast Names,* p. 157. Captain Walbran on p. 145 of this work says that Charles Dodd "commanded the *Beaver* 1843-1852, succeeding Captain McNeill"; but this would appear to be inaccurate.

[62] The Archivist of the HBC in a letter to the author concedes that this is so. He does not, however, rule out the

possibility that the solution of this minor mystery may yet be found in the voluminous HBC archives in London.

[63] The only evidence bearing on the question of which the author is aware is to be found in the following three passages in the *Letters of John McLoughlin* (second series, Champlain Society, Toronto, 1943; identical edition also published by the Hudson's Bay Record Society in London). It will be seen that it is difficult to disentangle from them the identity of the *Beaver's* commander in March 1843.

"In accordance with the arrangements made previous to our departure from Fort Vancouver, it will be necessary to allow Capt. McNeill to proceed to England in the *Cowlitz,* to sail from the river not later than the first week in October, next autumn, and I think that may best be done on the footing mentioned in the 51st par. of my dispatch of 1st inst., and I would recommend that the Steam vessel be put under the command of Captain Duncan, transferring Capt. Brotchie either to the *Prince Albert,* so as to take her home this autumn, or to the *Vancouver,* as you may consider advisable." (Simpson to McLoughlin, March 1, 1842. *Letters of John McLoughlin,* second series, p. 264.)

"On the 10 June the *Vancouver,* Capt. Duncan, sailed with the supplies for the trade of the North West Coast, and with the cargo of the *Valleyfield* belonging to the Russian American Company, and also that for them that came by the *Columbia,* she was first to proceed to Sitka, then to Stikine & Ft. Simpson, and requested Governor Etholine, to allow the Russian steamer to tow the *Vancouver* to Stikine, but the Governor more obligingly forwarded the supplies for Stikine by the Steamer, which returned in a few days, bringing the returns of Stikine to the *Vancouver* at Sitka." (McLoughlin to Governor and Committee, November 15, 1843, *ibid.,* p. 131.)

"Captain Duncan writes me, that on visiting the Forts of Tacow & McLoughlin, on his trip, with the Steamer, he found these Establishments exactly in the state they were left by our people, and the Indians particularly at Ft. McLoughlin very friendly." (McLoughlin to Governor & Committee, Nov. 18, 1843, *ibid.,* p. 176.)

[64] Douglas' personal diary for this period is in the Provincial Archives, Victoria. Considerable excerpts from it are given in my *Victoria: The Fort* (Mitchell Press, Vancouver, 1968). Several interesting articles on the founding of Fort Victoria are to be found in the *BCHQ* for 1943.

A Roman Catholic priest, Father Bolduc, was one of those accompanying Douglas, and his observations may be found in *Notices and Voyages of the Famed Quebec Mission to the Northwest* (Oregon Historical Society, Champoeg Press, Portland, 1956, pp. 193-4). I have given some excerpts from it in my *Victoria: The Fort* (pp. 51-53). Neither Douglas nor Father Bolduc gives the name of the *Beaver's* captain on this occasion.

5 In the service of civilization

With the founding of Fort Victoria in 1843, yet another chapter had been written in the history of the Pacific coast and of the *Beaver*. Many more chapters remained to be added to the story of both, but first the little steamer was to receive a new master in the person of Captain Charles Humphreys, who had been master of the *Columbia* since November 1837 and who took command of the *Beaver* in November 1844.[1]

However, he soon began showing signs of mental instability, and John Work was forced to report a serious incident to John McLoughlin:

> From the extraordinary and unaccountable conduct of Capt. Humphreys in leaving Fort Simpson as he did at midnight 19th Septr., only 12 hours before the time appointed to start, without orders and by stealth, leaving part of the stores, the despatches, and passengers behind, and afterwards putting the engineer Mr. Carless off duty and threatening to put him in irons, and placing John Flett, a man totally incapable, in charge of the engine room, thereby risking the destruction of the vessel and endangering the lives of all on board and other circumstances, there can be no doubt that the unfortunate man was labouring under a fit of insanity at the time, and had been less or more so effected (*sic*) at times for some time previous, though nothing occurred during his frequent visits to Fort Simpson to lead to suspicion of anything more than whims or eccentricity. His accounts were correct, he paid much attention to the business, and seemed proud of the success of the steamer's trade.[2]

Captain Humphreys was also apparently unreliable in other respects, admitting in response to questioning by senior officials of the Company "having been twice intoxicated since a Master Mariner in the Hon. Co.'s service, on both occasions after a safe arrival at Woahoo".[3] It was apparent that he was unfit to continue his duties, and he returned to England in the *Cowlitz* in the fall of 1845, not again to find employment with the HBC.

It was now necessary to choose a new commander for the steamer. McLoughlin, after considering both Captain McNeill and Captain Charles Dodd for the post, chose the latter, for reasons he outlined in a despatch to HBC headquarters in London:

> It is impossible to carry [out] your instructions in your 43d paragraph to place Capt. McNeill at the head of the Naval Department into effect, even if he had remained in command of the Steamer. As she never can come here he could not be in the way to perform the

The 'Beaver' in graphic art

The romantic career of the 'Beaver' and its importance in developing the economic and political life of the Canadian west has often inspired artists to represent it in various media.

The 'Beaver' in the Camosack Channel off Fort Victoria, 1846. A painting by A. S. Scott

The 'Beaver' heading west through the First Narrows of Burrard Inlet during the early years of its life on the west coast

At a coastal Indian village, probably during the 1860's. The two oil paintings on this page are by John Innes, a noted painter of western Canadian scenes.

A wood engraving from a special edition of the Vancouver 'World' issued to commemorate the tenth anniversary of the great Vancouver fire in 1886. This is possibly the first printed representation of the 'Beaver' and was obviously based on the lower photograph on page 31.

'Beaver' as it originally was, reconstructed in this 1915 ink drawing by H. P. Eldridge

An oil painting by an unknown artist. Painted on wood from the 'Beaver', it depicts the ship on the rocks at Prospect Point.

The wreck of the 'Beaver'. Oil on canvas by A. Lee Rogers

1891

1892

A series of pictures by Will Ferris, an early member of the B.C. Society of Fine Arts. He became secretary of the Art and Historical Association and later curator of the old Vancouver City Museum. The first painting, done about 1891, is a water colour, while the others in the sequence are sepia wash drawings.

1893

1894

duty. But Capt. McNeill applied to be allowed to remain in charge of a land Establishment, and as it is a matter of indifference whether he or Mr. Dodd commanded the Steam Boat, I acceded to his wish and appointed Captain McNeill to Stikine and Mr. Dodd to the command of the Steamer.[4]

Captain Dodd had served as second mate of the *Beaver* on its long voyage from England to Fort Vancouver, and had later been in charge of the HBC barque *Cowlitz*.[5] Born in Norwich in 1808, the son of John Beck Dodd, a surgeon, and Mary Cobbald Dodd, on November 22, 1842 he had married the daughter of John George McTavish and his common law wife Nancy McKenzie, by whom he was eventually to have seven children.[6]

The *Beaver* was active throughout this period, especially as it was now responsible for the business formerly done through the recently abandoned posts of Fort Taku and Fort McLoughlin. Chief Factor John McLoughlin was still unconvinced of the value of the steamer, and continued to press his views on his superiors. A letter from him to the Governor & Committee in this period did, however, show a more open mind on the question:

The Steam Vessel has a much larger trade than last year in consequence of the desertion of the posts of Tacow and Fort McLoughlin, the whole business of which is now managed through her. She has not made however so valuable a collection of furs as we formerly received when the two posts were also kept up, a decrease which may be accounted for in part by the growing scarcity of Beaver, & in part by the interference of the two Whale Ships which passed the winter at the port of Neweete near the north end of Vancouver's Island, and are reported to have made considerable purchases of skins from the Indians while the Steam Vessel was necesarily employed in carrying the Contract Otters to Sitka.[7]

Douglas, on the other hand, was well satisfied with the *Beaver,* noting in a letter to Simpson that whereas in 1842 it had taken in furs to the value of £819. 17. 1, in 1844 it had done business to the value of £5079. 2. 5. In both years, he noted, the fur trade along the coast had been worth about £16,000. He added: "I wish particularly to point out to you that Fort Simpson and the *Beaver* have collected nearly as many furs last season as were collected with a greater array of means in 1842".[8]

1844 saw a change in the management of the newly established Fort Victoria, as Charles Ross died apparently of appendicitis, on June 27, and was succeeded by Roderick Finlayson.[9] This period

The Oregon Treaty determines British and American possessions in the Northwest

(the exact date seems hard to determine) also saw another event which, though destined to have a connection with the *Beaver*, inevitably passed unnoticed at the time. Far away in Cornwall, a baby was born and given the name George Marchant; one day he would be the last captain of the *Beaver*.

The year 1845 saw the steamer busy about its duties, and so did 1846. This latter year, we should note, marked an important international development, as the Oregon Treaty finally fixed the boundary between British and American possessions in the Northwest.[10] Fort Vancouver was, as had long been expected, well to the south of the line. Thus it became necessary to plan the removal of the headquarters of the Company to a location farther north.

This did not take place just yet, however, and 1847 was a comparatively uneventful year in the area. It did see, though, the arrival at Victoria on March 22 in the *Cowlitz* of two men destined to serve on the *Beaver*. One was James Thorne, who was to be its engineer for a time. Although a competent man, he was inclined to be bad-tempered and to encourage discontent in others. He eventually returned to England in the *Norman Morison* in 1852, being replaced by a Mr. Johnstone.[11]

The other newcomer to Victoria on this voyage of the *Cowlitz* was Herbert George Lewis, destined later to command the *Beaver*. Born on January 2, 1828, the son of Edward Lewis, a gentleman farmer, he made several voyages to the Far East while still young. In 1846 he became the third officer of the *Cowlitz,* and arrived on it in Victoria in the spring of 1847. Later, he was to become the first officer of the *Otter,* which arrived on the Pacific coast in 1853, and eventually its captain. Not all his duties, however, were to be on board ship; he was for a time stationed at Fort Simpson, near the tip of the Alaskan panhandle, where he served under John Work.[12]

Meanwhile, important political changes were in the making, and the first few days of 1849 saw evidence of them. On January 13 the whole of Vancouver Island was granted by the Crown to the HBC, for a rent of seven shillings a year and a promise to bring out settlers to colonize it. In June, Douglas left Fort Vancouver and established his headquarters at Fort Victoria, all supplies at the former post being transferred to the latter.

The *Beaver* was laid up for a considerable time in 1849. Eden Colvile, recently appointed Associate Governor of Rupert's Land, reported that:

> The steamer is at present not in working

> condition, as the old boilers were worn out and have been removed. The new boilers were safely got in today, and as soon as she is ready for sea I shall take a trip in her to the Coal Mines, which appeared to be going on very successfully at the date of last advices from this place.[13]

The coal mines referred to were those at Fort Rupert on the northeast coast of Vancouver Island; their product was not of very high quality, but as the deposits at Nanaimo had not yet been discovered, the Company put considerable effort into developing them, and soon there was a small settlement at the place. Captain McNeill (who in 1848/49 had been in charge of Fort George at the mouth of the Columbia River) was in charge at Fort Rupert, though, as we shall see later, he was apparently not altogether aware of the differences between land and water discipline.

By early January, the boilers were finally installed, and Colvile reported to Sir J. H. Pelly, Governor-in-chief of the HBC:

> We took the trial trip on 11th & found that the engines worked well & that the steam was got up with a less expenditure of fuel than was the case with the old boilers.[14]

A month later, Colvile had further news to report concerning the Company's new venture at Fort Rupert:

> We left this place in the steamer *Beaver* on 16 ulto, and after sundry detentions from snowstorms reached Fort Rupert on the 22nd without accident & found the new boilers to work very well. We found everything at this establishment to be progressing satisfactorily. The stockades and bastions completed, several substantial buildings erected, and others in progress, and a portion of land cleared for planting potatoes. The Indians, about one thousand in number, who live around the fort have been all along well disposed and industrious, and I consider that the state of affairs here reflects great credit on Captn. McNeill's management — about 1100 tons of surface coal have been collected by the Indians, & are lying outside the Fort, properly protected from the weather, ready for shipment.[15]

A few weeks later, Vancouver Island welcomed, or at least received, its first governor, as Richard Blanshard, a young lawyer of 32 with no previous experience in colonial government, arrived at Victoria on H.M.S. *Driver* on March 11, 1850. His position was from the start to be an awkward one, as nearly every aspect of the life of Vancouver Island was under the firm control of Chief Factor

Trouble at Fort Rupert

James Douglas, and little remained for Blanshard to exercise his authority over.[16] He did, however, make intelligent reports to the Colonial Office concerning the resources of Britain's newest colony, and also recorded his suspicions of the all-powerful Company. On one occasion he sent to London for perusal a petition signed by Andrew Muir, one of the miners at Fort Rupert, protesting against Capt. McNeill's somewhat rigorous methods of management:

> I hereby charge the aforesaid William Henry McNeill, George Blenkinsop and Charles Beardmore that on Friday 3rd May 1850 at Fort Rupert aforesaid, the aforesaid William Henry McNeill, George Blenkinsop and Charles Beardmore did illegally assault my person. I likewise charge them that they did illegally imprison me from Friday 3rd May 1850 aforesaid until Saturday 15th of June 1850 and keeping me in irons and fed on bread and water during six days of the said period by which imprisonment I have sustained permanent and serious injury to my bodily health.[17]

The young doctor at Fort Victoria, John Sebastian Helmcken, took a trip on the little steamer, and in his old age recorded his recollections:

> The *Beaver,* a paddle-wheel steamer, was flush fore and aft and schooner rigged. In 1850 I was a passenger in this pretty vessel, Charles Dodd commander. She had the appearance of a small man-of-war, had four brass cannon, muskets and cutlasses in racks round the mainmast, and hand grenades in safe places. Along her sides were boarding nettings, and these could be triced up vertically or placed horizontally as the case required. She had an old-fashioned steering wheel, and her anchors and cables were always ready, as no wharfs existed on the coast in those days; carried plenty of hands, not only for defence but to cut wood for the furnaces, there being no coal in her early career. When leaving Victoria she was saluted by the fort with five guns, as it was a matter of policy to keep up the dignity of the Hudson's Bay Company not only at Victoria but at all the Company's posts along the coast to impress the Indians.[18]

Not all the passengers on the *Beaver* were adults. J. R. Anderson (1841-1930), destined to become in old age one of the last surviving links with old Fort Victoria, recalled how he and his companions at the settlement's first school were taken for a run in the steamer:

> My first experience of a steamer was when the *Beaver,* on her return from one of her periodical trips up north, came to an anchor in all the glory of bunting, Captain Dodd, first

The Americans seize the Beaver

and second officers, quartermaster, and the Lord knows how many of a crew besides. The occasion was taken advantage of by a general invitation to the school for an excursion in the Straits. So on board we went, being conveyed by the ship's boats. With what wonderment we looked upon all the arrangements in connection with this huge marine monster can better be imagined than described. The hissing of the steam, the whistling of the boatswain, the heaving up of the anchor, Captain Dodd on the bridge, which was amidships, giving orders, all gave us a thrill not to be forgotten. What a day of joy this occasion was.[19]

In the spring of 1851, because of difficulties with both the Company and his crew, Captain Dodd retired from the command of the *Beaver*;[20] this was not, however, the end of his association with the steamer, as he once again took command of it in the following year. In the meantime, Captain Charles Stuart became captain of the *Beaver* for a time.[21]

In the closing days of 1851, the *Beaver* became involved in a minor international incident. While engaged in towing the *Mary Dare* to Fort Nisqually, it called at Olympia for purposes of entry. There both ships were seized for an alleged breach of American laws; the captain of the *Beaver* was accused of "having permitted Mr. and Mrs. Work and family and Miss Birnie to land at Nisqually previously to the vessels being reported by the master at Olympia; and for having been entered in ballast when she had a few goods adapted for the coasting trade on board".[22]

The *Mary Dare* was freed on bond, but the *Beaver* remained in American custody for several weeks. The American authorities eventually ordered the return of the seized goods, but the HBC felt it had suffered a loss of potential revenue from the incident, and claimed compensation. Eventually a mixed commission, composed of British and American officials, decided that the Company was entitled to $1000.[23]

1852 saw a renewed interest in the area's natural resources. A large deposit of high quality coal was discovered near Nanaimo, setting in motion the economic growth of that region. Meanwhile, Captain McNeill took the *Beaver* to the Queen Charlotte Islands to look for the gold ore they were rumored to contain, but with no success.[24] The *Beaver* also took to Sitka the "Contract Otters", i.e., those promised to the Russian authorities in exchange for trading rights in the Alaskan panhandle.

Some time in 1852 Captain Dodd, his difficulties

The Christmas Hill murder

with the Company apparently resolved, resumed command of the steamer, a post he continued to hold for the next four years.

It was now evident that the steamer was fulfilling the hopes placed in it, and this was signalled by the decision of the Governor and Committee in London to have a sister ship built and sent out to the Pacific coast. This was the *Otter,* of 287 tons, which was to arrive from the United Kingdom in 1853. Colvile when he heard of this new development gave it his hearty approval:

> We consider the determination you have come to respecting the screw vessel for the service of the Northwest Coast very judicious, as vessels propelled when necessary by steam power are much more adapted for the navigation of the Straits and Inlets in that quarter than sailing craft. It is not, I suppose, intended that she should depend wholly on her steaming powers, but only use the engines during calms or adverse winds.[25]

Late in 1852 an unexpected event took place whose consequences were eventually to require the services of the *Beaver.* The Company had a large sheep farm at Lake Hill (also called Christmas Hill), a few miles north of Victoria. Two shepherds, Peter Brown and James Skea, looked after the flocks. On the morning of November 5, 1852, Skea discovered the body of Brown, who had been shot by an unknown assailant. Before long, Governor Douglas had learned through his close contacts with the native tribes that Brown had been killed by two Indians, one a Cowichan and the other the son of a Nanaimo chief. He quickly organized an expedition, consisting of H.M.S. *Thetis,* under the command of Captain Augustus Kuper[26], and the HBC vessels *Recovery* and *Beaver.* The little flotilla, carrying 130 seamen and marines plus eleven half-breed servants of the HBC, left Victoria on January 4, 1853, reaching the mouth of the Cowichan River on January 6. The next day Douglas and his party went ashore, where

> a small tent was pitched for the Governor, where were deposited presents for the tribe, besides his pistols and cutlass, the use of either to depend on circumstances.[27]

The tribesmen, who had put on their full war-array for the confrontation, were inclined to be hostile, and certainly not to surrender the culprit, considering that a payment in goods would be sufficient to compensate for the crime. The young lieutenant who witnessed the scene still remembered half a century later how the white men were faced by:

over two hundred tall warriors, their height exaggerated with head-plumes, faces terrifically painted with red ochre, decked with loin-ropes of shells which met their deer-skin leggings and clattered with every movement as they leaped from the canoes.[28]

Douglas himself in a subsequent report to the secretary of the HBC outlined in matter-of-fact language the tense scene:

> On landing they made a furious rush towards the point which I occupied, a little in advance of the Force, and their demeanor was altogether so hostile that the marines were with difficulty restrained from opening a fire upon them. When the first excitement had a little abated, the murderer was brought into my presence and I succeeded after a good deal of trouble in taking him quietly into custody; and sent him a close prisoner on board the steam vessel. This capture having removed all cause of dispute, I assembled the Indians and spoke to them long and seriously on the subject of their relations with the Colony, and the rules which must govern their conduct in future. They expressed the utmost regret for the misconduct of their countryman, and their desire to live on friendly terms with the Colony, and appeared much intimidated by the imposing force before them. They left us in course of the afternoon in the best possible temper, and the Forces were immediately afterwards re-embarked, having fortunately concluded the day's work without firing a shot in anger; though several times, on the very point of coming to a serious rupture, which indeed could not have been prevented had the discipline of the troops been less perfect; and my orders not been rigidly enforced by Lieutenant Sansum, who on all occasions gave me the most hearty and cordial support.[29]

The ships then proceeded to Nanaimo, where Douglas again encountered opposition to his demands, finding

> a decided reluctance on the part of the tribe to surrender the murderer; they however at length consented to deliver him into our hands; but on the day appointed they failed in their promise, and made an attempt to ransom his life by a payment of furs. In consequence of that breach of faith, I took his father and another influential Indian into custody, in hopes of inducing them by that means to bring in the criminal; my object being if possible to settle the difference without bloodshed and without assailing the tribe at large. After two days of the most anxious suspense, it was again arranged that they should bring the criminal to the vessel, and he was accordingly brought to with-

Vancouver Island's first jury deliberates aboard the Beaver

> in half a mile of the anchorage; but on seeing me repair to the spot, he was landed and fled to the woods. There being then no alternative except a recourse to coercive measures, without a positive loss of character, I ordered an immediate advance towards the River, near the mouth of which the Nanaimo villages are situated. We accordingly pushed rapidly in that direction, but from the shallowness of the water, the boats grounded about three quarters of a mile below the first village where the troops were immediately landed, and we pushed rapidly towards it, and before the Indians had recovered from their first consternation we succeeded in carrying the stockade without firing a shot. We spent the night there, and the boats came up before morning.
>
> We then moved up the River, to the second village which we found nearly deserted by its inhabitants, who had fled with their property to the woods. The murderer's father was chief of this last village, consisting of many large houses and containing all their stock of winter provisions. They were now completely in our power, and as soon as I could assemble a sufficient number of the inhabitants, I told them it was my intention to treat them as enemies unless they submitted to the demands of justice.[30]

Learning that the murderer was hiding in the nearby woods, a force was despatched to search for him, and soon was close on his trail.

> The track led to a large stream and was lost, to be regained on the snow-covered boulders higher up, and then came a stretch of deep water, which it was agreed that the fugitive must have crossed by swimming. Reaching the shallow water, they struck the trail once more, and at last in an open glade they ran him to earth, hidden under the roots of a fallen tree, and so brought him, bound and wearied, to the stockade.
>
> It was pitiful enough to see the splendid wild man captive among his own people. What they felt I know not; what they evinced was the stoical indifference of their tradition. Not a sound was uttered, not a look showed pity or anger as we closed round our prisoner and set off on the return march.[31]

A jury was then empanelled on the *Beaver* (the first ever convened on Vancouver Island) and, since the prisoners admitted their guilt, its verdict was not in doubt:

> They were sentenced to be hanged, and the execution took place in the presence of the whole tribe, the scene appearing to make a deep impression upon their minds, and will I trust have the effect of restraining others from crime.[32]

The death of John McLoughlin

Thus in firmly establishing the principle that crime would not go unpunished, the *Beaver* had played its part. Douglas himself assessed with accuracy the outcome of the expedition:

> The surrender of a criminal, as in the case of the Cowegin murderer, without bloodshed, by the most numerous and warlike tribe on Vancouver's Island, at the requisition of the civil power, may be considered as an epoch in the history of our Indian relations which augurs well for the future peace and prosperity of the Colony.[33]

The next few years were comparatively uneventful ones for the little steamer. The *Otter* arrived in the northwest in 1853, and was usually assigned the longer voyages, the *Beaver* being generally confined to Puget Sound. A man destined to serve in both ships arrived on the Pacific coast in 1856; this was Captain Thomas Pamphlet, born in Barking, Essex in 1835 or 1836, who had helped transport supplies to the Crimea during the war with Russia; a future captain of the *Beaver,* he was soon given the post of second mate on the *Otter,* its commander at this time being Capt. Herbert Lewis, and its chief mate John Swanson, both also eventually to command the *Beaver*.[34]

It is interesting to note that the *Otter* became for a brief period a warship. The outbreak of the Crimean War in 1854 found British possessions in the northwest almost defenceless, and Douglas, after appealing unsuccessfully to London for armed assistance, hastily armed the crew of the *Otter,* numbering about thirty. Actually, an agreement had been reached at the highest level between the two great fur companies that in the event of war they would not molest each other's posts, but it was some time before Douglas was informed of this.[35]

The Crimean War came to an end in 1856,[36] and with it the danger of hostilities involving the northwest. In the winter of 1856-1857 a new set of boilers was installed in the *Beaver,* which after being laid up for a time because of this, resumed her accustomed duties.

As it happened, 1857 saw one event which, though once it would have caused wide reverberations, passed almost unnoticed. On September 3 at Oregon City, John McLoughlin, for some years retired into private life, breathed his last. Though his final days with the Company had been unhappy, his place in history was secured, for just as his one-time subordinate James Douglas was eventually to be known as "the father of British Columbia", so McLoughlin is known today as "the father of Oregon".

Gold!

The death of the "white-headed eagle," as the Indians called him, was to mark a dividing line between two eras; for now the northwest, especially the area comprising southern Vancouver Island and the lower Fraser River, was about to undergo an extraordinary and almost instantaneous transformation. Gold was discovered in the interior of what would soon be named British Columbia, and miners from California, hearing of the rich new strikes, poured northward to make their fortunes. Victoria was their first stopping-place; from here the treasure-hunters, having bought supplies, crossed the Gulf of Georgia as best they could, and made their way up the valley of the Fraser. The *Beaver* (which by this time usually burned coal) travelled back and forth frequently between Victoria and Fort Langley, and miners often made use of her services. Its captain in the period 1856-1858 was usually John Swanson, who, born in 1827, had arrived on the Pacific coast from England in 1842, and had seen service on both the *Cadboro* and the *Vancouver* before commanding the *Beaver*.[37] The voyage took from twelve to fifteen hours, and was far from comfortable, but those who believed themselves about to discover the riches of El Dorado were doubtless in no great mood to complain. The less favored argonauts were crossing the Gulf of Georgia in rowboats and canoes, with many agonizing experiences.

One traveller in this period, however, a Charles Woodard, has left a rather candid account of his experiences of discomfort as a passenger on the *Beaver:*

> We stood huddled together for mutual warmth on the afterdeck like cattle, and indeed with less provision for our comfort than is nowadays provided for cattle. A small awning covered but half the deck passengers, and afforded but little protection against a heavy driving storm of sleet and snow which followed us from start to finish. Fortunately the only redeeming feature of the trip was its brevity, but it was long enough to impress a lasting memory of its discomforts, and it stands unrivalled as the smallest voyage with the largest amount of discomfort in all my experience on salt water.
>
> However the little steamer possessed the merit of staunchness, and she certainly proved as industrious as her patronymic, for she kept steadily buffeting head winds and a very heavy sea until she landed us, drenched, cold, and hungry, but withal thankful, at Fort Langley.[38]

Before long, it was evident that the days when the mainland held only the native Indians and a few trading-posts were rapidly ending. Though some of the gold-miners returned empty-handed to California in disgust, many thousands remained, and small communities quickly sprang up along the Fraser. Soon there was a need for government, not only to preserve law and order, but to establish beyond doubt that the vast area between the Rockies and the Pacific Ocean was a possession of the British crown; no one was more alive to this necessity than the energetic and far-seeing Douglas, now for seven years the Governor of Vancouver Island, as well as a Chief Factor of the HBC. Without waiting for guidance from distant London, he set about asserting his authority and that of the British Government.

In May 1858 he issued a proclamation, asserting the sole right of the HBC to trade with the natives, and threatening to confiscate all vessels and goods found on the rivers without a license from the Company and permission from the customs officials at Victoria. The force at Douglas' disposal was small indeed, but by sheer force of character he successfully bluffed his way through.

Still the miners came on, and as Douglas' urgent despatches reached London, describing the amazing transformation taking place, the authorities there took action. In the summer of 1858 the House of Commons passed a bill creating the colony of New Caledonia, a name which, when it was realized that a French colony in the south seas already bore that name, was soon changed to British Columbia; Douglas was then informed by the Colonial Secretary, Lord Lytton, that if he would sever all connections with the HBC, he could reasonably expect (in addition to remaining Governor of Vancouver Island) to be made the first Governor of British Columbia. Douglas promptly accepted this offer—indeed, so sure had the British government been that he would, that the authorities had sent him his commission before they had received his acceptance; there remained now only the formal ceremonies inaugurating the new political entity.

In November 1858 Douglas journeyed to the mainland. He had a variety of means of transport at his command, but he was clearly anxious that on this historic occasion, the little craft that had brought him to Victoria that March day fifteen years before should not be slighted. Both the *Otter* and the *Beaver* were dispatched to the mainland, but Douglas transferred from the *Otter* to the *Beaver* shortly before ascending the river. The *Otter,* a speedier craft, arrived first at Fort Langley, but it was the *Beaver,* the more historic vessel, which brought the new colony its first governor.

British Columbia is born, 1858

On November 19, 1858, in the main hall of the HBC at Fort Langley, Douglas administered the oath of office to Matthew Baillie Begbie[39] as first judge of British Columbia; Begbie then swore in Douglas as Governor; and Douglas in turn read a proclamation ending the Company's exclusive trading rights on the mainland. A new era had begun, and once again the *Beaver* had assisted at its birth.[40]

The next year saw an addition to the HBC fleet as the *Labouchere* arrived on the Pacific coast. This was a much larger vessel than the *Beaver* (680 tons and 202 feet long). Built in England in 1858 of teak and Baltic oak, and capable of ten knots, it was brought out to the New World by Captain John F. Trivett, arriving at Victoria on January 31, 1859. Captain John Swanson was then placed in command of it, yielding the bridge of the *Beaver* to Captain J. L. Sinclair. Named after the Rt. Hon. Henry Labouchere, Secretary of State for the colonies from 1855 to 1858, it was to continue active in these waters for several years,[41] until its loss in 1866. In that year it was refitted, and under the command of Captain Mouat[42] assigned to carrying the mail from Victoria to San Francisco. On its first voyage, however, it hit a reef on April 14, 1866 near the latter port and sank with some loss of life.

Captain Swanson had not long been in charge of the *Labouchere* when, with no effort on his own part, he was involved in a bizarre political career of almost meteoric brevity. In 1859 the Nanaimo seat in the House of Assembly became vacant, and a man named Barnston was elected to it. Governor Douglas, however, disapproved strongly of him, and under his stern eye Barnston felt himself quail; though he got as far as entering the House, he promptly resigned, declaring himself unworthy of the honor. Douglas then called a new election; a Captain Stewart was pronounced the only qualified voter, and he promptly in turn elected Captain Swanson to the Assembly. The latter, however, was absent on his duties in the *Labouchere,* and was much surprised to learn on his arrival that he was now a member of the Assembly. He, too, however, in turn declared himself unfitted for the position, and resigned, much to the annoyance of the Governor.[43]

1859 also saw the death on February 28 of a former commander of the *Beaver*. William Brotchie, born in Caithness, Scotland in 1799, had had a career with the HBC which included service on the *Dryad* and command of the *Cadboro, Nereide* and *Cowlitz*. He had also been in charge of the *Albion*

The War of the Pig

in 1849 when it ran onto a reef near Victoria, which in consequence later received the name of Brotchie's Ledge. After an unsuccessful attempt at operating a timber business at Fort Rupert, he had been appointed harbor-master of Victoria in 1858. Here, despite the many duties which fell to his lot in the busy days of the gold rush, he had found time to become an ardent member of the Victoria Pioneer Cricket Club. The *Colonist* in its obituary of March 5, 1859 [which, curiously enough, makes no mention of any connection between Capt. Brotchie and the *Beaver*] described him as "a portly, good-natured, even-tempered man", and many years later Dr. Helmcken was to recall him as "genial, heavy, fat, with twinkling humor".[44]

1859 also found Governor Douglas facing another serious crisis, as the question of the ownership of San Juan Island in the Gulf of Georgia came close to involving Britain and America in war. Douglas, with the approval of the British Government, had always maintained that the island was a British possession, and the HBC had maintained for some years a thriving farm there. A pig from this farm caused some damage to the garden of an American settler in the area, whereupon the American shot the pig and the Company demanded compensation. Higher circles of authority were appealed to, and eventually the Americans decided to cut the Gordian knot by occupying the island with troops. Accordingly on July 27, 1859, Captain Pickett of the American army, with sixty soldiers, landed on San Juan.

Douglas wavered between two possible courses of action — a prompt counter-blow and acquiescence in a fait accompli. In order to gain a trustworthy account of the situation on the island, he despatched his son-in-law, A. G. Dallas,[45] now in charge of HBC operations in Victoria, to the scene in the *Beaver*.[46] Eventually, mainly as a result of strong pressure from high officers of the British navy stationed at Esquimalt, Douglas decided reluctantly on a cautious policy, and a joint occupation of the island was agreed upon, British troops landing peacefully on San Juan on March 20, 1860.

In the meantime, the *Beaver* had been refitted. Returning from San Juan, it had struck a rock and suffered damage, the *Colonist* for March 24 reporting the accident as "knocking off some copper and injuring her keel". Now its upper works were extended and its passenger accommodation improved, the *Colonist* of March 27, 1860 remarking that "the little vessel looks well in her new dress".

A victory for the Beaver

Perhaps in response to a feeling of well-being engendered in its sturdy timbers by these changes, it now took part in a race from Victoria to New Westminster with the American stern-wheeler *Julia,* commanded by Captain Bushnell. The *Colonist* of April 3, 1860 gives some details of the contest:

> An exciting race between the steamers *Beaver* and *Julia* took place on the last trip to New Westminster. Both vessels having been recently repaired, and their machinery thoroughly overhauled, the race was a test of their speed. From the moment the *Beaver* sighted the *Julia* off Trial Island, the *Beaver* (although the oldest steamboat on the Pacific coast, and drawing ten feet of water and unable to take advantage of the shallows out of the influence of the tide) never allowed the *Julia* to gain an inch on her, and arrived at her destination (Holbrook's wharf, New Westminster) 35 minutes before the *Julia.* We understand that considerable money changed hands on the occasion.

A few weeks later the *Beaver* was able to add insult to injury as its defeated rival

> was towed into the harbor yesterday morning by the *Beaver* for repairs.[47]

A former captain of the steamer was from time to time in the news. The Victoria *Gazette* for March 26, 1859 carried a letter complaining that:

> Several persons have been bitten by the savage dogs belonging to Capt. Dodd. Scarcely a person passes along Government Street, in front of Capt. D's house, without these dogs flying out at him, and attempting to insert their teeth in his flesh. Complaint has been laid before Mr. Justice Pemberton, but he is pleased to take no notice of the matter. Is there no remedy for this dangerous nuisance?

A few days later, another letter by the same aggrieved citizen reported that the offending canines had been killed by their owner, and the affair was thus closed.[48]

On May 21 of the same year there was a further reference to Capt. Dodd in the columns of the *Gazette*:

> The substantial mansion on Government Street, formerly the residence of Captain Dodd, has been removed from its original site to a position a few rods further north, on a line with the street, forming a corner at the junction of Government street with a new avenue opened through to Broad street. The building whose removal we have noted is, we are informed, to be occupied by a branch banking house of the North British Bank, as soon as some necessary alterations in the interior are made.

A replica and a model

Completed in 1966 to commemorate the union of the two colonies of Vancouver Island and British Columbia, this replica was displayed in waters sailed by its original over a hundred years earlier.

Though there are several models of the 'Beaver' in existence, this recent reconstruction by André F. Christoffersen of the Maritime Museum of B.C., Victoria, is probably the most accurate and finely detailed.

The Beaver *suffers a setback*

An interesting if somewhat grisly story in which Capt. Dodd figured prominently was carried in the columns of the Victoria *Colonist* late in 1859. The Captain had at one time been a warm friend of a Col. Ebey; the latter had been killed on Whitby's Island (in the San Juan group, not far from Victoria) by an Indian during the troubles in the American northwest in 1857, and his scalp had been kept by members of the tribe at a place about 750 miles north of Victoria. Captain Dodd had previously attempted to purchase the relic of his dead friend, but with no result. However, after further negotiation, and the payment of a sum of money, the natives were persuaded to return the scalp, and Capt. Dodd brought it back to Victoria on the *Labouchere*. The *Colonist* for November 29 furnished a few details:

> The scalp is entire, with all the hair and ears. The skin is free from fleshy matter, appears white, but slightly discolored with smoke. The beautifully fine silken brown hair is as natural as when struck down by the ruthless tomahawk of the savage.
>
> One of the sad mementoes of border life.

In the summer of 1860, however, Captain Dodd was suddenly taken ill at Port Simpson. He was brought down to Victoria by Captain Swanson in the *Labouchere,* and died on June 2, being buried in the Quadra Street Cemetery. The *Colonist* a few days later gave a summary of his career:

> Capt. Charles Dodd, for the last twenty-six years an employee of the Hudson Bay Co., expired at his residence near St. John's church, on Saturday afternoon last. Capt. Dodd came first to this country on the old steamer *Beaver,* which was the first steam vessel to paddle in the great Pacific Ocean, in the year 1835, in the capacity of second mate; and from his correct business habits and irreproachable character, soon gained the esteem and confidence of the Company, and had risen step by step until he occupied the honorable position of Chief Factor for the Northwest Coast. Capt. Dodd was a native of Norwich, England, and was aged 51 years; he leaves a loving wife and four children to mourn his loss. The funeral will take place today at 11 o'clock, A.M.; the services will be conducted by the Rev. Dr. Evans at the Wesleyan Methodist Chapel on Cormorant Street.[49]

At almost the same time that the *Beaver* was losing one of its former captains, the little steamer itself was undergoing the first serious setback in its career. The HBC agreed in return for a payment of $1000 a month to withdraw it from competition with private commercial interests in the Gulf of

Sir George Simpson dies, 1860

Georgia, the *Colonist* for May 22, 1860 reporting briefly that:

> The steamer *Beaver* has been bought off the route between here and New Westminster. An increase in the price of freight may accordingly be looked for.

The same issue of the *Colonist* that described the funeral of Captain Dodd also noted a change of employment for Captain Lewis:

> Capt. Lewis, late of the *Beaver,* succeeds Capt. Swanson in the command of the *Labouchere.*

From time to time, other names connected with the vessel were in the news. September 1860 saw two events, one trivial, one momentous, which recalled the earlier days of the northwest's first steamer. The *Colonist* reported on September 27 that:

> Miner Martin, grocer on Humboldt Street, appeared in court yesterday morning with his left eye in mourning, and preferred a complaint against William H. McNeill for assaulting him on Saturday evening last on Humboldt street. McNeill was convicted and ordered to pay a fine of five shillings and fourteen shillings costs.

Meanwhile, on the other side of the continent, the man whose far-seeing vision and inflexible will had brought the *Beaver* into being had come to the end of his days. Sir George Simpson's health had deteriorated, and he was unable to attend the annual Council of the HBC at Fort Garry, being forced to turn back at St. Paul. He clung to life, however, and lived to enjoy one final hour of glory. The Prince of Wales (the future King Edward VII) was touring North America, and in the late summer of 1860 his barge, accompanied by canoes manned by Iroquois warriors in full regalia, paid a ceremonial visit to Simpson's estate at Isle Dorval, three miles from Lachine. Simpson entertained his royal visitor in style, and thus the one-time illegitimate child whose very date of birth is unknown at last reached the inner circle of distinction. But it was an honor he did not live long to enjoy; he had come to the end of his strength, and on September 7 he was dead.

The *Beaver* still lay idle in the harbor at Victoria, and continued to do so until late in 1862. For a time it was used as a convenient place to store explosives, which resulted in some correspondence between Governor Douglas and Captain Richards of the Royal Navy. Neither was unduly anxious to see the town (which was to become a city in 1862) brought down around his ears, and eventually the gunpowder in the steamer was transferred elsewhere.

The Beaver *joins the Senior Service*

Meanwhile, the British Admiralty was beginning to take a renewed interest in this remote part of the world, and had decided that the Pacific coast should be more thoroughly surveyed. There had been a previous survey by Captain Richards in H.M.S. *Plumper* and *Hecate,* and the Admiralty now decided to allow £3500 toward continuing this work, directing the captain to secure some suitable vessel for the task. He recommended the *Beaver,* but found that the HBC was asking £4000 per annum for the rent of it. Richards was able to negotiate an agreement by which Governor Douglas agreed to pay the difference between the two figures out of the treasury of the colony. All parties were thus satisfied, and the work of converting the *Beaver* to a survey ship was then commenced.

By late in 1862[50] the work was largely finished, the White Ensign replaced the HBC flag; the *Beaver* was then towed from Victoria to Esquimalt by the gunboat *Grappler* for her final fittings and tests. On April 11, 1863, the *Colonist* had an article on what was now to be officially known as "Her Majesty's Hired Surveying Vessel Beaver":

> This vessel, which only awaits the arrival of the mail steamer, by which some surveying instruments from England are expected, will probably sail for the scene of its labors about Monday or Tuesday next. Since being chartered by the Government for surveying purposes she has been thoroughly overhauled and repaired, and her present condition reflects no small credit upon the officers under whose auspices the metamorphosis had been effected. On her trial trip she steamed eight and a half knots, but her capability is set down at nine; her engines being rated at 70 horse power. A convenient apartment upon the upper deck has been appropriated for use as a chart room, abaft of which is the stateroom of the master. The cabin of the vessel is now devoted to the general use of the officers as a ward-room, while the engineers' and surgeon's state-rooms are situate in the starboard and port paddle-boxes respectively. The following is a list of the officers belonging to the vessel. Mr. D. R. Pender, Master Commander; Mr. E. R. Blunden, Second Master; Dr. Bogg, surgeon, naturalist, etc. and Mr. Charles Bonwick, Engineer in charge. Her crew consists of twenty-nine seamen and one marine. They are provided with their small arms and accoutrements, but the only piece of ordnance (if worthy to be considered as such) borne by the vessel is a 1 lb. swivel gun forward.[51]

By June 1863 the *Beaver* was ready for sea, and it sailed from Esquimalt to begin serving in a new role the communities of the Pacific coast of British North America.[52]

Its first task was to touch at various settlements on northern Vancouver Island, including Fort Rupert and Nanaimo. It found all quiet and it then proceeded to Texada Island, concerning which Colonel Moody, commander of the Royal Engineers in B.C., had requested information regarding its mineral resources.

The following year (which also saw the retirement of Governor Douglas from public life and the dismantling of the last remnants of old Fort Victoria) it surveyed Nekwilta Inlet on the mainland, and later Queen Charlotte Sound. Then after a short period in Victoria while its boilers were repaired, it examined the mouth of the Fraser at the request of Governor Seymour. As a result, Capt. Pender recommended that a system of permanent buoys and beacons should be established to mark the channel. Later in the year it brought despatches to Captain Gilford of H.M.S. *Tribune,* asking him to send a gunboat to Bentinck Arm, where an Indian uprising was feared. No outbreak occurred, but meanwhile the *Beaver* was used as a supply vessel, taking provisions to H.M.S. *Grappler,* which for a while maintained a patrol in Bute Inlet.

In 1865 the *Beaver* was again active, surveying Knight's Inlet, Queen Charlotte Sound, and also Broughton and Johnstone Straits. It was at this time that Seymour Inlet was named after Douglas' successor as governor of B.C.

We might note that the *Beaver's* sister ship, the *Otter,* was also active at this time. The *Colonist* for May 17, 1865 reported that:

> The H.B. Company's steamer *Otter,* Captain Swanson, arrived yesterday from a trading expedition around the Island, having been absent for 17 days. Messrs. Buttle and Hooper, who were despatched by the government to make a cursory prospect in different localities, with a view to ascertaining the most advisable spot for future exploration, were on board.

1866 was another busy year for the *Beaver,* as many channels between the north end of Vancouver Island and latitude 54° 40″ were explored. The mouth of the Fraser was not, however, neglected, as it was discovered that the channel of the river was changing. For a time the *Beaver* was also at Bella Bella, where relations with the Indians remained tranquil. Its sister ship, the *Otter,* was also not idle in this period. The *Colonist* for May 28, 1866 reported that under the command of Captain Lewis, it had arrived in Victoria from Stikine with 2000 gallons of oil, 16 bales of furs, 7 additional cases of furs, and about 6000 deer, goat and sealskins. Meanwhile, a Pilot Board was constituted in Victoria, its first three members being Capt. Swanson, Capt. Cooper and the Hon. J. A. Homer.[53]

1867 was not, however, altogether one of smooth steaming for the *Beaver*. It was towed by the gunboat H.M.S. *Forward* from Esquimalt to Victoria, where it was forced to await the arrival of new boilers from England. In July, while Confederation was being celebrated in the eastern part of British North America, it underwent a thorough examination, its timbers being found as sound as the day it was launched. Indeed, it was discovered while it was being refitted that as a result of running aground earlier near Race Rocks a ten-pound rock had embedded itself in the steamer's timbers without producing significant damage, surely a tribute to the sturdiness of the craft.

The refitting was duly completed, but before the ship put to sea again a moment of indignity was to befall it. While coming down the ways, something went wrong and it ended on its side on a mud-flat. It was pulled off by H.M.S. *Forward,* and after recovering its breath and self-composure set off for Fort Simpson in the northern mists.

1867, we might note, was the year which first saw an association between the *Beaver* and the man who was in due course to become its last captain. George Marchant, born in Cornwall in 1844, had joined the Royal Navy in 1858. In 1866 he left Plymouth on H.M.S. *Zealous,* arriving in Esquimalt in July 1867. Later in the same year, he became a member of the *Beaver's* crew, and soon afterwards the steamer visited Alaska.

1868 was another active year, as parts of the coast as far distant from each other as the Portland Canal and the mouth of the Fraser were surveyed. The following year, suitable locations were found to place beacons on Spanish and Sturgeon Banks at the mouth of Burrard Inlet. The needs of local sawmills were in the minds of those in charge, and it is interesting to note that a few years later the *Beaver*, by then itself a tow-boat, was to make use of the very guides which it had been responsible for establishing.

One incident which took place in 1869 is worth recalling. During the breakfast hour one day, the crew of the *Beaver* were resting on the rocks facing the waters of Hecate Strait. A breaker which persistently appeared in the same place caught Marchant's attention. He reported the matter to

The HBC flag is raised again over the Beaver

Lt. Coglan, and upon investigation it was found that the cause of the breaker was a dangerous rock off the shore; as a result of this discovery, Captain Pender gave it the name of Marchant Rock.[54]

The *Beaver's* last year as a survey ship was 1870. During it, Beecher and Pedder Bays at the eastern end of the Strait of Juan de Fuca were charted, and with these tasks completed, it became time to return the vessel to its civilian owners. December 21 saw the paying-off ceremony in James Bay, as Captain Pender and Lt. Coglan handed the ship back to Chief Factor James A. Grahame and Capt. Herbert Lewis, the representatives of the H.B.C. The white ensign fluttered down, the HBC flag was run up; another chapter in the life-story of the *Beaver* was ended.[55]

By now, the century was two-thirds over. The world was changing; ships much larger and more modern than the *Beaver* were in service on the Pacific coast; and one might have expected that the little steamer would before long pass into the shadows. But this moment was not yet; it still had good service to give, and for nearly two more decades the waters it had first entered in 1836 were to hear the sound of its paddles. It is to this closing phase of the *Beaver's* career that we now turn.

Footnotes

[1] *Letters of John McLoughlin,* second series, p. 392.

[2] Work to McLoughlin, Oct. 24, 1845. *Letters of John McLoughlin,* third series, p. 145.

[3] *Letters of John McLoughlin,* second series, p. 392.

[4] *Letters of John McLoughlin,* third series, pp. 30-31.

[5] Captain Walbran, in his *British Columbia Coast Names,* says that Charles Dodd "commanded the *Beaver* 1843-1852, succeeding Captain McNeill" (p. 145); but this is apparently inaccurate.

[6] These children were:
Mary Grace; married John Kriemler on October 23, 1862. Kriemler, who was Swiss, came to Victoria in 1862 and formed a partnership with Joseph Spratt in an iron works on Store Street. He later operated a farm at Strawberry Vale. He was chief of the Victoria volunteer fire department for a time. About 1880 he went to Guatemala, where he made a large sum of money in coffee. He died in Germany in 1889, leaving a widow and two children. Kriemler, like Capt. McNeill, was one of those who signed the annexation petition of 1869. (See W. E. Ireland, "The Annexation Petition of 1869," *BCHQ,* Vol. IV, No. 4, October 1940.) Another signer, it is interesting to note, was Chief Trader John Swanson, commander of the *Labouchere* and the *Otter.*
Charles John; died in London in 1891, aged 43. (See *Colonist* for May 21, 1891.)
Elizabeth Ann; born Nov. 30, 1845. Married Robert Williams Dec. 23, 1860 (*Colonist,* Dec. 29, 1860). Her husband was drowned off Rose Spit in 1877.
Edward James; born about 1851.
Roderick Finlayson; born Dec. 3, 1853. He was for a time employed as manager of the HBC store at Masset, Q. C. I., and was on his way to see his wife, who was seriously ill in California, when he was involved in a train accident in Oregon. He died as a result of his

injuries in hospital at Salem, Oregon, in Dec. 1890 (*Colonist,* Dec. 9, 1890.)
Dugald McTavish
Henry Work; born Jan. 2, 1860. Died in London June 28, 1921. His son, Charles Edward Dodd, attended Harrow and Balliol, and had a career in the British Foreign Office.
Captain Dodd himself died on June 2, 1860. See *Colonist* for May 29 and June 5, 1860.

[7] McLoughlin to Governor & Committee, Nov. 20, 1844, *Letters of John McLoughlin,* third series, pp. 51-52.

[8] Douglas to Simpson, March 5, 1845. *Letters of John McLoughlin,* third series, p. 182.

[9] A monument to Ross was unveiled in the old Quadra Street Cemetery (now Pioneer Square) on June 27, 1943, the 99th anniversary of his death, by his grandson, Mr. Francis Ross.

[10] Some uncertainty still existed regarding some of the Gulf Islands, which was not cleared up until 1872.

[11] On July 21, 1852, Eden Colvile reported to the Governor & Committee in London that "the engineer Mr. Johnstone who replaced that exceedingly troublesome person Mr. Thorne has so far conducted himself satisfactorily." (*London Correspondence Inward from Eden Colvile* 1849-1852, Ed. E. E. Rich, Hudson's Bay Record Society, London, 1956, p. 144.)

[12] Named after Captain Lewis are Lewis Rock in Baynes Passage, Lewis Channel in Desolation Sound, Lewis Point in Beaver Cove, Broughton Strait, Lewis Rocks in Queen Charlotte Sound, and Lewis Island in Arthur Passage, Kennedy Island. Mary Basin, Nuchalitz Inlet, Nootka Island was named after his wife by Capt. Richards of the *Plumper* in 1859 (Walbran, *Op. Cit.,* p. 304.)

[13] Eden Colvile to Sir J. H. Pelly, October 15, 1849. *London Correspondence Inward from Eden Colvile* 1849-1852, p. 5.

[14] Colvile to Pelly, Jan. 14, 1850. *Ibid.,* pp. 14-15.

[15] Colvile to Pelly, Feb. 6, 1850. *Ibid.,* pp. 16-17.

[16] For an account of Blanshard's troubles, see my *Victoria: The Fort* (Mitchell Press, Vancouver, 1968) pp. 75-96.

[17] Blanshard, Despatch No. 16, June 10, 1851.
There was trouble of another sort at Fort Rupert in this period. While the *Beaver* was there, three of its crew deserted, hoping to join the brig *England,* which was then loading coal for California, where no doubt they hoped to become gold-miners. While hiding in the near-by woods, they were killed by Indians. So suspicious was Blanshard of the HBC that he suggested to the British Government that the Company had been responsible for their deaths. In a later despatch he retracted this suggestion. (See Despatch No. 5 (August 18, 1850) and Despatch No. 7 (Oct. 19, 1850).)

[18] Quoted from an article "S.S. Beaver's Romantic Story" by Bruce McKelvie in the *Vancouver Province* for April 12, 1925. I have not been able to trace the quotation, but it also occurs in Captain Walbran's article on the *Beaver* (*British Columbia Coast Names,* p. 40).
In the *Colonist* holiday number for Christmas 1887, Helmcken recalled a few other details. "She had a large crew — active, robust, weather-beaten, jolly good-tempered men — fat from not being overworked — some grey, some grizzled, some young; the former had once been similar to the latter in the service."

Dr. Helmcken, born in London of German parents in 1824, arrived in Victoria on the *Norman Morison* in 1850, and was soon appointed a magistrate at Fort Rupert by Governor Blanshard. On Dec. 27, 1852 he was married by the Rev. Robert Staines to Cecilia, daughter of Governor Douglas. in 1856 he became speaker of Vancouver Island's first House of Assembly, a position he held for many years. In January 1885 he was chosen as the first president of the B.C. Medical Association. He died in Victoria on Sept. 1, 1920 and is buried in Pioneer Square. His house, built in 1852, still stands and is open to the public. For some details of its construction, see my *Victoria: The Fort,* p. 107.

[19] Anderson, Notes and Comments (unpublished MS in PABC), pp. 179-180.

A letter in the Victoria *Colonist* of August 27, 1903 by Anderson gives some more details of the steamer:
"The young *Beaver,* a side-wheel steamer, had no top hamper, no cabins or awning over the deck. Her deck was flush . . . Having plenty (of) hands, the *Beaver* looked like a gentleman's yacht, every knob or gun polished, the deck likewise; in fact, everything, berths and cabins included, were as clean as elbow grease could make them, a creation of beauty and pride in our eyes.
Indians are or were stoical, possibly did not show any surprise at seeing the *Beaver,* but simply squatted on their haunches and grunted. They are said to have believed that the vessel carried a fire devil below or ran by witchcraft."

[20] Colvile to Simpson, January 14, 1850. "Dodd has sent in his notice of retirement, partly because he was not promoted, and partly because he cannot agree with Thorne the Engineer." (*London Correspondence inward from Eden Colvile 1849-1852,* p. 190.)

[21] "In the spring of 1851 McNeill initiated the new captain of the *Beaver,* Charles Stuart, into the trade and navigation of the coast." (*Letters of John McLoughlin,* third series, p. 318.)

Captain Charles Stuart was born in Bristol in 1817. In 1859 he served for a time as a magistrate at Nanaimo, but without giving general satisfaction (see Victoria *Colonist,* Oct. 10, 1859). Later he established a trading post at Ucluelet. He died on Dec. 19, 1863 while on board the sloop *Red Rover* off Sangster Island, and was buried in the old cemetery at Nanaimo (*Colonist,* Dec. 30, 1863).

Named after him are Stuart Point, Protection Island, Stuart Anchorage in Grenville Channel and Stuart Island in Haro Strait (Walbran, *British Columbia Coast Names,* p. 475).

[22] See *London Correspondence Inward from Eden Colvile, 1849-1852,* p. 136.

[23] The award was made on Nov. 29, 1854, and was to be paid before Jan. 15, 1855. See the "Report of the Mixed Commission on Private Claims," compiled by Edmund Hornby, London, 1856, pp. 212-214.

[24] Colvile to Governor & Committee, July 21, 1852. *London Correspondence Inward from Eden Colvile,* pp. 143-144.

[25] Colvile to Governor and Committee, July 21, 1952. *London Correspondence Inward from Eden Colvile,* p. 162.

On May 14, 1852 Herbert George Lewis (later to command the *Beaver*) was appointed first officer of the *Otter.*

[26] Captain Augustus Kuper was in these waters 1851-1853. Kuper Island in Stuart Channel was named after him by Capt. Richards of H.M.S. *Plumper* in 1859. Captain Kuper later took a prominent part in forcibly opening Japan to the commerce of the world in September 1864.

His daughter, Mrs. Adams Beck, became under the pen-name of E. Barrington a prolific composer of historical romances about such figures as Lord Byron and Lady Hamilton. She lived in Victoria for many years, and died Jan. 3, 1931. (See *Colonist,* Jan. 7, 1931, p. 7.)

[27] Admiral John Moresby, *Two Admirals,* London, John Murray 1909, p. 126.

[28] *Ibid.,* p. 130.

[29] Douglas to Barclay, Jan. 20, 1853. PABC.

[30] Douglas to Barclay, Jan. 20, 1853.

[31] Moresby, *Op. Cit.,* pp. 134-135.

[32] Douglas to Barclay, Jan. 20, 1853.

[33] *Ibid.*

[34] For more information regarding the Pamphlet family, see Early Vancouver, unpublished MS by Major J. S. Matthews; copies in Vancouver City Archives and Provincial Archives, Victoria. Volume V, pp. 198-202.

[35] See "The war scare of 1854; the Pacific Coast and the Crimean War," *BCHQ*, Vol. V, No. 4, October 1941, p. 250.

[36] A future captain of the *Beaver,* George Rudlin, born in Essex, England in 1836, had served on the transport *Victoria* in this war. He came to the Pacific coast in 1856. See Lewis and Dryden, *Marine History of the Pacific Northwest,* Antiquarian Press, New York, 1961, p. 120.

Bruce McKelvie, in an article in the Victoria *Times* for May 11, 1935, states that "in 1856 she was borrowed by the American authorities in Washington to transport soldiers to fight against the Indians," but I have not been able to find any confirmation of this statement. A letter by the author to the HBC Archivist in London elicited the reply that "extracts from the records which we have regarding the *Beaver* at various dates in 1856 give no indication of her undertaking any extraordinary duties during the year."

[37] Swanson Bay was named after him by Captain Dodd about 1844; Swanson Channel was named by Capt. Richards of the *Plumper* in 1859, and Swanson Island by Capt. Pender of the *Beaver* in 1867. (Walbran, *British Columbia Coast Names,* p. 480.)

Captain Swanson would appear to have had some deficiencies. Judge M. B. Begbie, in a letter dated March 12, 1859, reported that "the complaints about him are loud, bitter and universal; and only soothed by the explanation that he is insane." (Begbie Papers, PABC.)

[38] Charles McCain, *History of the S.S. Beaver,* Vancouver, 1894, pp. 48-49.

[39] For an account of Begbie's background, character and career, see four articles by Professor Sydney Pettit in the *BCHQ* for 1947. Some additional sidelights on him may be found in my *James Douglas: Servant of Two Empires* (Mitchell Press, Vancouver, 1969).

[40] On December 24, 1858, Douglas reported from Victoria to Lord Lytton: "In consequence of the return of mild weather, the ice on Frazer's River has broken up, and vessels are again plying with goods and passengers between this place and Fort Langley. The steamers "Santa Cruz" and "Beaver", lately returned from thence, with upwards of 300 passengers from the mining districts, and, as reported on good authority, 7,340 ounces of gold dust, exclusive of the sums in the hands of miners." (*Papers Relative to the Affairs of British Columbia*, Part Two, London, 1859.)

On March 25, 1859 Douglas again wrote to Lord Lytton: "I fancy that gold will be found in many other parts of the coast of British Columbia. Mr. McNeill, the officer in charge of the Hudson's Bay Establishment at Fort Simpson, latitude 54° 25 N. in a letter just received from him, makes the following observation:—"You mention that some adventurers will visit this quarter (Fort Simpson) in search of gold, and in my opinion they will find it, as it has been found even in this harbour." (*Ibid.*)

[41] On August 2, 1862 it was suddenly captured by a band of Taku and Sitka Indians while on a trading expedition. The situation was very tense for some time, but after a long parley, the Indians were persuaded to leave the ship. See Lewis and Dryden, *Marine History of the Pacific Northwest,* p. 83.

[42] Captain William Alexander Mouat was born in London in 1821, and came out in 1845 as second mate of the brigantine *Mary Dare.* At various times, he was in command on the *Otter, Enterprise* and *Labouchère.* He died while travelling in Knight's Inlet on April 12, 1871 and is buried in the Quadra Street cemetery. (Walbran, *British Columbia Coast Names,* p. 344.)

[43] See Victoria *Colonist* for June 12, 1955, p. 11. Whether this "Captain Stewart" is Captain Charles Stuart, one-time captain of the *Beaver,* is hard to determine with certainty, but it seems very likely.

[44] *Colonist,* May 30, 1897.

[45] Dallas was born at Berbice, British Guiana on July 25, 1816, and married Douglas' daughter Jane on March 9, 1858. They spent their honeymoon on San Juan Island. In 1861 Dallas succeeded Sir George Simpson as Governor of Rupert's Land (i.e. all the Hudson's Bay Company's territories in North America) and left Victoria with his family to take up his duties at Fort Garry. He died on Jan. 2, 1882.

[46] See Bancroft, *History of British Columbia 1792-1887,* San Francisco, 1887, p. 616.

[47] *Colonist,* April 21, 1860.

[48] Savage dogs seem to have been a feature of captains of the *Beaver.* The *Colonist* for July 19, 1866 was to report: "A man named Clarke complained yesterday of having been assaulted by Captain Pamphlet. The quarrel arose, as is too frequently the case lately, about a ferocious dog, the property of defendant. The dog having attacked the complainant, he resorted to the use of bad language towards the animal. His owner, Captain Pamphlet, was fined $5, and the Magistrate administered to complainant (who also owns a dog that he allows to run at large) and defendant a severe lecture on the impropriety of endangering the public safety by not properly securing the animal."

Captain Pamphlet, it is perhaps worth noting, was born at Barking in Essex.

[49] *Colonist,* June 5, 1860. For an account of the funeral, see the *Colonist* for June 7. Capt. Dodd had seven children, of whom at least five were alive at this time. Dr. W. F. Tolmie became the guardian of Dodd's children.

[50] The *Cadboro* was lost in October of this year (see *Colonist* for Oct. 8, 1862).

[51] A letter by J. R. Anderson, one of Victoria's earliest pioneers (1841-1930) in the Victoria *Colonist* for February 24, 1927 provides the following summary of the changes undergone by the *Beaver* during its career: "When leased to the Imperial Government to complete the hydrographic survey left unfinished by H.M.S. *Plumper,* she was completely transformed by the removal of her rigging, which was replaced by two pole masts to be used for signalling purposes. Deck houses for the accommodation of the officers and crew were erected on her decks and the steam whistle installed which, needless to say, she was not provided with originally. In the third stage of her existence her appearance as a tug was again completely changed by the removal of her two pole masts, which were replaced by a short pole in her bow for carrying a light. It may be added that part of this pole is that erected at Brockton Point under the impression that it is part of the original mast of the *Beaver.*"

[52] For an interesting account of the *Beaver's* work as a survey vessel, see the article "H.M.S. Beaver" by Lt-Commander Laurence Farrington, R.N. in the *Beaver* for Spring 1961, on which much of the following is based.

There is a picture of the *Beaver* as a survey ship in the *Colonist* for May 21, 1924.

[53] Victoria *Colonist,* June 16, 1866.

[54] Walbran, *British Columbia Coast Names,* p. 320.

[55] Among the geographical features named after those on board the *Beaver* in this period were Pender Island, Coglan Rock and Anchorage, Bonwick Island and Blunden Island. Not all those thus commemorated were human beings. Connis Point on Redonda Island, Connis Rocks in Chatham Sound and Connis Inlet in Beaver Passage were named after the ship's mascot, a Skye terrier named Connis.

We might also note Wootton Bay, Lancelot Arm, Malaspina Inlet, which was named by Capt. Pender about 1863 after Henry Wootton, clerk of writs of the Supreme Court of Vancouver Island and later post-master of Victoria. His grandson is Judge R. A. B. Wootton.

6 Into the sunset

The next few years were comparatively uneventful ones for what was now affectionately called "the old *Beaver*." Some of its former commanders were from time to time in the news. On February 22, 1870, for example, the *Colonist* reported that Capt. Lewis, now commander of the *Otter,* was soon to return to Victoria from London with a bride; his choice was the daughter of Capt. E. E. Langford, one of Vancouver Island's pioneer settlers, who had since returned to England.[1] August 30, 1871 saw the birth at Victoria of a son to Capt. Thomas Pamphlet and his wife (the widow of a HBC trader named John Cotsford). This son was later to become Capt. Frederick W. Pamphlet, and to have a distinguished career in B.C. waters, commanding such ships as the S.S. *Badger* and the Canadian National Steamship *Prince Rupert*.[2] On October 22, 1872, the *Colonist* was forced to record the untimely death of a former captain of the *Beaver*:

> It is once more our painful duty to chronicle the death of a prominent citizen. Captain John Swanson, so well known and so much thought of by everyone who knew him, has gone to his long home. A week ago today he was at his post as usual and took the steamer *Enterprise* up to New Westminster, returning with her on Wednesday. On Thursday last a renewal of his former illness came on and the doctors were of opinion that the attack would prove fatal. On Friday evening he was not expected to last the night out, but not till yesterday morning at 1:30 o'clock did he succumb.
>
> Captain Swanson (who was aged about 45) was a native of Rupert's Land. He joined the Hudson's Bay Company's service at the age of 14 and two years after came out as apprentice in the H.B. Co's ship *Cadboro*. He assisted in clearing away the brush to build the old Hudson Bay Company's fort and stockade . . . In him the Company has lost an honest and faithful servant and one whom they will not easily replace. The flags at the Government Buildings, City Council Chambers and those of many citizens were flying at half-mast yesterday out of respect to his memory.

Meanwhile, George Marchant had temporarily abandoned the sea, and, like so many others in this era, was elsewhere in search for gold. This was apparently not so rewarding as he had hoped, for after a year or so he accepted the command of the steam coaster *Union*. This vessel was at least unusual; it was basically a scow driven by an engine transplanted from a threshing machine, could do only four or five knots, and had no reverse.

In 1874 came a great change for the *Beaver*. The

Company which had owned it for so long evidently decided that it was no longer an economic asset, and sold it to a group of Victoria citizens for $17,500.[3] One of them, Captain George Rudlin, assumed command of the vessel. Born in Essex in 1836, he had had a varied and interesting career. At the age of twelve he had joined the crew of a fishing smack out of Colchester, England; later he had worked on the Newcastle colliers, and later still on the steamship *Victoria,* then engaged in transporting supplies to the British army fighting in the Crimea. Venturing into the other hemisphere, he had sailed on the brig *London* for Valparaiso, and later in the *Red Gauntlet* had reached San Francisco in 1856. Esquimalt first saw him in 1859, and in 1860 he had settled on Discovery Island (where Rudlin Bay is named after him), buying the schooner *Circus* and later building the *Discovery,* using them to carry wood and coal between the ports of the Gulf of Georgia. One of the first cargoes of the latter ship was lumber from the Port Madison mills, which he took to W. P. Sayward's yard in Victoria, part of it being used in the construction of the first Presbyterian Church in that city. Later he was in charge for three years of the *Black Diamond,* which carried coal from Nanaimo to Victoria. Two other ships, the *Emma* and the *Grappler,*[4] had Rudlin for their captain; he was thus well acquainted with the B.C. coast, and soon proved a capable commander of the *Beaver*. The *Colonist* for October 20, 1874, noted that "the tug *Beaver,* Capt. Rudlin, sailed for Nanaimo yesterday to tow down the bark *Whistler,*" but otherwise records of the steamer for this period are scanty.

Other figures once associated with the *Beaver* were from time to time brought back to the public's attention. Capt. Lewis was taking the *Otter* up and down the coast, sometimes as far north as Wrangel. The *Colonist* for November 22, 1871 had reported on one voyage from Port Essington to Victoria in terms that might have seemed to some readers a non sequitur:

> The passengers who came down by the *Otter* are enthusiastic in their praise of Capt. Lewis and his brave little boat. The living freight was packed like sardines in a box.

So ecstatic, indeed, were Capt. Lewis' passengers at this treatment that they presented him with an address

> for his kind consideration, and as the boat neared the wharf stentorian lungs and throats

The death of Captain McNeill

sent forth three hearty cheers for the *Otter* and her gallant officers and crew.

On October 13, 1874, the *Colonist* again reported on the *Otter,* noting that it had brought down from Alaska $200,000 worth of gold dust, including a 16-ounce nugget, one of the biggest ever seen in Victoria. Once again, the passengers, no doubt largely successful miners, were eager to furnish Capt. Lewis with a testimonial.

From 1872 to 1874 another former captain of the *Beaver,* W. H. McNeill, though now well advanced in years, had been commanding the *Enterprise*, but in the closing months of the latter year he relinquished its command to Captain Lewis.[5] The *Enterprise,* indeed, was to prove the last command for Capt. McNeill. On September 3, 1875 at his family home on the shores of McNeill Bay, he died of heart disease. The *Colonist* reported him as being 74 years of age, but it seems likely that he was actually 72. The estate which he left was considerable, but the complexities of his will were later to result in considerable litigation, which was not settled for several years.

Captain Thomas Pamphlet was also from time to time in the public eye. In 1860 he had taken Captain Edward Stamp and Gilbert Sproat in the schooner *Meg Merrilees* to Alberni, where they had established a sawmill; in 1864 he had taken Stamp to Burrard Inlet and helped him select the site for what was later known as the Hastings Mill.[6] In 1867, along with Captains Gardner and Titcomb, he had been appointed a pilot for the ports of Victoria, Esquimalt, Burrard Inlet and Nanaimo,[7] and a few years later, he was on occasion to command the *Beaver.*[8] On December 18, 1874, however, the *Colonist* recorded that:

> Pilot Pamphlet, whose licence was revoked by the Pilot Board for being absent from duty without leave, brought the matter before Judge Gray yesterday. The judge decided that the Board had exceeded its authority and Mr. McCreight, Q.C., who appeared for the Board, said his clients would publish in the next Saturday's *Gazette* an order rescinding the revocation.

A year later, on Dec. 8, 1875, the same paper was obliged to record less welcome news for Captain Pamphlet:

> The licence of Thos. Pamphlet as a pilot of British Columbia was yesterday annulled by the Pilot Board, for putting the steamship *City of Panama* on Beaver Rock.[9]

A few weeks later, another former commander of

The wreck of the 'Beaver'

The 'Beaver' on the rocks at Prospect Point, about 1891

A side view, not too long after the grounding — probably 1888-89. Most of 'Beaver's' deck fittings are still intact.

The ship has been damaged but not yet extensively plundered. The nameboard is present and the wheel is intact, with a lot of rope still evident. The picture is hard to date, but by the quantity of marine growth below the high water mark, the 'Beaver' should have been on the rocks for about two years — that is 1890.

Destruction by souvenir hunters is now under way. The nameboard has fairly recently been removed and the hand grips on the wheel cut off. About 1890-91

Scavenging is well advanced. Nearly all signs of the position of the nameboard have gone. The wheel, previously hacked at, is no longer visible, and practically all the rigging has gone. Note the man at the rear of the port paddle box, and a second just appearing over the top of the deck house.

Going fast. The boiler has broken away from its original position, changing the angle of the smoke-stack. 'Notices', possibly warnings to vandals or of danger, have been posted.

'S.S. Yosemite' — the ship that finally sent the 'Beaver' to the bottom

The interior of the engine room showing the boiler in the background and the shaft of the port paddlewheel at the right of the picture

The last vestiges of the historic steamer — its boiler and the port paddle are all that remain visible of the 'Beaver'.

'A tug and a freighter'

the *Beaver* went to his long rest. This was Captain William Mitchell, a native of Aberdeenshire, who had first come to the Pacific coast in 1836 or 1837, and had successively been in charge of the *Vancouver, Cadboro, Recovery, Una* and *Beaver*. At the time of his death he was about 74 years of age, and the Victoria *Colonist* of January 14, 1876 in reporting his death the day before declared that:

> No one was more popular in this community both with young and old, than the deceased gentleman, who had always a kind word for everybody, and very many indeed will for a long time miss his familiar form and his cheery greeting in the streets.[10]

The *Beaver,* however, continued to be a familiar sight in the coastal waters of B.C. (which since 1871 had been a part of the Dominion of Canada). On November 4, 1876, the *Colonist* reported that:

> The steamers *Beaver* and *Gertrude,* which have been actively engaged during the past season in Stikeen River traffic, will be hauled on the ways and thoroughly repaired for the requirements of next year's trade in the same locality.

Shortly afterward, the *Beaver* was given an official government inspection. The report classified it as "a tug and a freighter," 41 years old, with oaken hull, and two engines each with a 36″ cylinder. The stroke was 36 inches, and the ship was fitted with two square boilers, each ten feet long, made of ⅝″ plate. These boilers had been built in 1867 by Low, Muir and Baudsley of London and were of the return tubular type. The hydro pressure allowed was 19 pounds, with a working pressure of 12 pounds.[11]

All this was apparently quite satisfactory, for the *Colonist* for November 24 reported that:

> The steamer *Beaver* will leave here this morning for Nanaimo, to tow down the bark *Wellington,* coal laden for San Francisco.

The following year, 1877, saw substantial changes for the *Beaver,* as it was given a major refit[12] and passed under the financial control of Capt. J. D. Warren, who was also for a time to be its commander; others with a financial stake in the *Beaver's* earnings were Henry Saunders, a Victoria grocer, and Benjamin Madigan, its chief engineer.

Warren, born in Prince Edward Island in 1837, had arrived in Victoria in 1858 and by 1864 had begun trading along the B.C. coast in the *Thornton.* In March 1868 he had been involved in a dramatic series of events. The schooner *Growler,* out of Puget Sound, was wrecked in the Queen Charlotte Islands and its crew were all either drowned or killed by the local Indians. By way of retaliation, in a battle in June of the same year, Warren killed twenty natives of the area.[13]

In this year, too, John Fullerton became the vessel's second engineer; a young man then, he was to become in the course of time one of the last living links with the little steamer, and to recall in his old age how it took from morning to dusk to go from Victoria to Burrard Inlet.[14] A report on the ship in October 1877 described it as having two engines and a cylindrical return tubular boiler eleven feet long, while its hydro pressure was set at 30 pounds and its working pressure at 20; it generally carried a crew of ten.

An enterprising though somewhat poetical writer for the *Colonist* was moved in its issue of October 27, 1877 to extol the sturdy little craft:

> What have we here — skimming with the grace and swiftness of a sea-bird over the surface of the harbor and making the water boil and surge in her wake in great foam-laden swirls? A strange-looking steam craft, truly, with rapidly revolving wheels set well forward, and with rakish funnel emitting a volume of intensely black smoke. Friend, that strange looking craft is the *Beaver* — the pioneer steamer — the first steam vessel of any class that disturbed the placid waters of the wide expanse of water known as the Pacific Ocean. She was built of live oak just 42 years ago at a Thames shipyard, came round the Horn the same year, ascended Columbia River under steam in the spring of 1836; brought the late Sir James Douglas[15] to Vancouver Island to locate and found the future metropolis of British Columbia, and has performed more hard work than any vessel now afloat, and now converted into a tow-boat is as sound as a dollar and in better condition than ever for active service. She has just left the Albion Foundry with a new boiler and modern improvements to her machinery, has made the run from the wharf in Victoria to Esquimalt harbor, passed round the Royal Squadron lying at anchor there, and as we write is returning to her wharf at Victoria, having occupied only one hour and eight minutes in the trip. Captain Dug. Warren looks proud of the craft he commands, and Mr. Madigan, the obliging engineer, under whose supervision the improvements were perfected, informs us that the live-oak timbers and frame of the *Beaver* are as sound as the day on which they were placed in her hull.

The same paper only three days later was forced, however, to report an accident to the steamer.

Captain George Marchant commands the Beaver

While towing the *Henry Buck* to Nanaimo the vessels were caught in the tide of Dodd Narrows and collided. The smoke-stack of the *Beaver* fell off and it was almost disabled by damage to one of its paddle-wheels. However, it was towed to Victoria, where repairs took only a few days, and it was then able to resume its duties. In this period these consisted mainly of towing coal ships to and from Nanaimo and lumber carriers to and from Burrard Inlet. Sometimes it waited at Albert Head for vessels inward bound from Cape Flattery; it also on occasion towed booms of logs and transported cattle. Once it took fifty Chinese to Alberni where they had hopes of finding gold; their success or lack of it is not recorded, but at least they, or a similar party of their countrymen, gave its name to China Creek.

During this period the *Beaver* acquired a new captain. This was John F. Jagers, born May 29, 1851 in Memel, then part of East Prussia. His grandfather had lost his life fighting for Napoleon, and his father earned his living buying livestock from the farmers of eastern Europe and fattening the animals for slaughter. To the end of his days the young Jagers remembered his father haggling with the local peasants, then still dressed in their colorful old-world costumes.

However, the boy soon decided on a life at sea, and at about the age of thirteen an uncle took him for a voyage, carrying timber from the Baltic to London on the barque *Johanna* in 1865. Later, he sailed to other parts of the world, arriving in the course of his travels at Victoria in 1878 as second mate of the *Gondolier*. He then left this ship and signed on as mate of the *Beaver* under Captain J. D. Warren. Two years later he succeeded to its command, and for three years was engaged in the towing and general freighting business. During this period, while helping with the building of a schooner in Captain Warren's shipyard, he caught his right arm in a circular saw, being laid up for five months, and sustaining permanent injuries to one hand.

1878 was a comparatively uneventful year for the *Beaver*. In this year George Marchant (who had been its mate in 1876 and 1877) became its captain, and was soon towing ships into Nanaimo and Burrard Inlet.

1879, however, saw an incident which reflected that age was creeping up on the *Beaver*. The steamer

Fire aboard the Beaver

Empire ran aground near Active Pass; the *Beaver,* summoned for assistance, failed to pull it clear, and a larger tug-boat, the *Alexander,* had to be called in to perform the task.

The *Beaver's* owners, however, still thought her good for some time yet; this was shown by an advertisement in the *Colonist* for October 5, 1879. It drew the attention of "ship owners and captains" to the fact that:

> The powerful steam tug *Beaver,* fitted with two 36-inch cylinders, having been thoroughly overhauled and fitted with new boilers and other improvements, making her one of the most powerful and economical tugs on this coast, is now prepared to tow vessels in B.C. waters. For further information, apply on board to Captain J. D. Warren at Dickson-Campbell's wharf or to Henry Saunders, Johnson Street.

This year was marred by a misfortune for a former commander of the *Beaver,* Captain McNeill's farm house being almost completely destroyed by fire on February 3.[17]

In 1880 there was a fire aboard the *Beaver* itself, and its upper works were damaged; it successfully surmounted this crisis, however, and continued to give good service.

1880 was also the year of the "Thrasher Case." The *Thrasher,* a new American sailing ship engaged in carrying coal from Nanaimo to San Francisco, struck on Gabriola Reef while being towed by the *Beaver* and the *Etta White,* and was a total loss (July 14, 1880). As the *Thrasher* was not actually attached to either tow-boat at the time of the accident, much litigation resulted in an effort to assign responsibility.[18]

The following year the *Beaver* was towing logs in Puget Sound, where Eugene Thurlow at times gave assistance as a pilot in these difficult waters; he was to become one of the last living links with the steamer, being able to reminisce about it as late as 1953, when he was a hale and hearty ninety-four.[19]

In the spring of 1883 the *Beaver* was again in trouble — apparently quite critical trouble. The *Colonist* for February 13 reported the details:

> On Saturday, the old *Beaver,* the first steamer that clove the waters of the Pacific, ran full tilt at a rock near the entrance to the first narrows of Burrard Inlet and soon filled and sank. The telegraph states that the steamer is down by the head, with her stern resting on the fatal rock and the hold full of water. It is believed she can be raised with the assistance of camels

lashed to her sides, as the hull is very strong, being built of British oak which is as strong as the day on which it was first cut. The *Beaver* has had many experiences with rocks during her long career in these waters. On one occasion, when in the service of the British Admiralty, she struck a reef near Race Rocks and actually carried away a piece of the rock, which months afterwards was found embedded in one of the timbers. The Burrard Inlet rocks will scarcely succeed where those of the Fuca Straits failed. The *Beaver* is owned by B.C. Towing and Transportation Co., and is uninsured.[20]

It was not yet, however, the *Beaver's* time to go, and she was refloated, though the accident, by strange coincidence, was a forerunner of fate at that same harbor entrance.

Two months later Captain Jagers was again in the news. He was no longer in command of the *Beaver,* having assumed the direction first of the tug *Pilot* and later of the steamer *Grappler.* On April 28, 1883 the *Grappler* sailed from Victoria with a cargo of supplies for a cannery, carrying about a hundred passengers, most of them Chinese employees of the canneries along the coast. While off Duncan Bay, fire was discovered in the hold, and although preparations were quickly made to fight it, the flames soon gained the upper hand.

It was obvious that they could not be extinguished, and Captain Jagers attempted to head the vessel toward the shore. Unfortunately, the wheel ropes had been destroyed by the fire, while the engines were still driving the ship in circles, and thus fanning the flames. Adding to the confusion was the panic of the passengers which hampered the launching of boats. Even when several boats were got into the water, they immediately sank under the weight of those jumping into them. However a few survivors were landed on Valdez Island.

Meanwhile Captain Jagers remained on board until the forward deck fell in, leaving him with only a few feet of planking near the stern. Then, with his face and hands severely burned, he jumped into the icy waters and succeeded in getting clear of the sinking craft. His plight was doubly dangerous as he had not until that moment learned to swim. Eventually an eddy deposited him on a large boulder, where he then lost consciousness. Fortunately he was found soon afterwards by some local residents and given artificial respiration. The total losses in the disaster will never be known, but have

The old ship falls on hard times

been estimated as 19 white, 68 Chinese and 2 Indians.

When he had recovered from his harrowing experience, Captain Jagers was again given command of the *Beaver.* An item in the Victoria *Evening Post* for September 11, 1883, gave some details of his exacting duties:

> The steamer *Beaver,* Captain Jagers, arrived from Chemainus about 5:30 last evening, towing what was probably the largest boom of logs ever seen either here or on the Sound. It measured 100 feet in width and was 800 feet long . . . The Beaver left Chemainus on Thursday morning last, but had to anchor two nights, owing to the thick and foggy weather. She reached the entrance to this harbor yesterday afternoon, without a single mishap or the loss of a log. Some little difficulty was experienced in steering the mammoth raft into the harbor, two men being stationed on the structure for that purpose; but Capt. Jagers succeeded in skillfully navigating his cumbersome tow, and bringing it to its destination at Rock Bay, near Sayward's sawmill.

Times had meanwhile become less prosperous, and the *Beaver* was now laid up for four long years. The onward sweep of events continued; the little settlement on Burrard Inlet, once known as Gastown and later as Granville, but now called Vancouver, was incorporated as a city on April 6, 1886 and on June 13 of the same year destroyed by fire. It was almost immediately rebuilt, however, thus demonstrating that, like the *Beaver,* it was not easily daunted.

Vancouver was of course still minute compared with the metropolis on the southern tip of Vancouver Island, yet its rapid recovery from almost total destruction had been a sign that a new age was dawning. There were soon to be others: on May 23, 1887 the first transcontinental railroad train reached the city, while on June 21 the first trans-Pacific steamer, the *Abyssinia,* arrived there from Hong Kong. The world was now girdled by a continuous chain of transportation — the famous "All Red Route" around the globe — and the knot had been tied in the Pacific northwest.

Thus the chapter that had opened with the arrival of our little steamer at Fort Vancouver in the spring of 1836 was closing. The political future of the various parts of the northwest had been settled,[21] confederation from sea to sea was a reality,[22] the fur trade had yielded to farming, manufacturing and mining, the old days and the old ways were vanishing. The *Beaver's* task was done.

The last voyage of the Beaver

Yet there would be a few months of service. The vessel was licensed to carry passengers, and began running between the numerous logging camps on Burrard Inlet. George Marchant was the captain, Charles Morris the mate, and David Symmons (or Simonds) the Chief Engineer; William Evans was the assistant engineer and his brother Thomas Evans a deck-hand. John Brownlee and Benjamin Collis were the firemen, while P. Clitto and Thomas Smith were the coal-passers. The cook, of Celestial origin, rejoiced in the simple, though one hopes inaccurate, appellation of "One Lung."

The *Beaver*'s last voyage was made on the night of July 26, 1888.[23] About some of the details of its final hours afloat there is still dispute, which it is now too late to resolve.[24] However, there seems no reason to question the account given on February 19, 1941 to Major Matthews, Vancouver City Archivist, by W. H. Evans, the assistant engineer of the ship on its last trip:

> She had been running north, and this time, the night she was wrecked, it was dark, about one a.m. in the morning, we were going to Nanaimo for bunker coal before going north to some island, Harwood or Thurlow Island, and from the time we left the dock until we were on the rocks was not very long, I think I was having a sleep, and don't actually know who was on board except the crew, or if there were any except the crew.
>
> Anyway, I think the tide was pretty near high water, but still running in, because the captain hugged the shore pretty tight to get past the eddy off Observation Point, and the first thing I knew she hit, and that settled it. We all got off. We were in too much of a hurry to pack up, and, believe me, it would not have taken any of us three minutes to pack up, because in those days we travelled light. We all got off into the water and waded ashore; walked through the park to the Sunnyside Hotel, and we were at rest and peace. There was a peaceful calm settled down on us. The bar-keeper, when he saw us, thought we had gone nutty because we had not long before left the bar-tender with goodbyes, and promised we would see him again, by and by, but he did not expect to see us that quick.[25]

Regardless of exactly how it had got there, the *Beaver* was now fast on the rocks near Prospect Point. Nor was it promptly pulled off; on the contrary, it was to remain there for four long years, while swarms of the curious came to gaze at it, many of whom removed what they could of it for souvenirs.[26] Numerous photographs were taken of it, some of which show stately liners, outward bound for the broad Pacific, passing not far from the old steamer where it lay stranded on the rocky beach — the old and the new, saluting each other speechlessly.

1889 came and went, and 1890 and 1891.[27] The busy city of Vancouver became busier; trains from the East were now a commonplace. By the summer of 1892, everything removable had been taken from the wreck, including the last remnants of its dignity; yet still it lay on the rocks.

Then a chance of a better fate for a moment made an appearance. The organizers of the world's fair held at Chicago in the summer of 1892 to commemorate the 400th anniversary of the sailing of three famous ships — the *Nina,* the *Pinta* and the *Santa Maria* — had heard of the old *Beaver* and recognized its historic importance. They began to negotiate for the purchase of what was left of it, and it seemed as if it was to enjoy a final hour of triumph before the eyes of curious thousands.[28] But the fates decided that it had earned a last long sleep, away from the madding crowds. One day, June 26, 1892, the steamer *Yosemite,* passing at full speed near the wreck with a high neaptide running sent a larger wave than usual toward it; it was enough to dislodge the hulk from its resting-place and send it sliding down towards the bottom, there to rest to this day in twenty fathoms of swiftly-flowing water. Almost exactly a century after Captain George Vancouver had sailed into Burrard Inlet in the *Chatham* and the *Discovery,* the long and notable story of the busy little *Beaver* apparently was ended.

Footnotes

[1] For an account of Langford's ways and works, see "The trials and tribulations of Edward Edwards Langford" by Prof. S. G. Pettit, in the *BCHQ* for 1953. Mrs. Lewis died in Victoria in 1903. Another of Langford's daughters, Emma, married John Bull, master of H.M.S. *Plumper*, on Feb. 7, 1860 (*Colonist,* Feb. 14, 1860), but the bridegroom expired on November 14 of the same year, being buried in the Quadra Street Cemetery. (Pioneer Square).

[2] Captain Thomas Pamphlet's other children were Capt. Thomas H. Pamphlet, jr., Capt. Robert Pamphlet, Kate Pamphlet and Mrs. T. Provis of Ladysmith, V.I. Captain Thomas Pamphlet, jr. apparently died about 1916, and Capt. F. W. Pamphlet on November 11, 1951 in the North Vancouver General Hospital at the age of 80. Capt. Robert Pamphlet had an interesting career in the 1920's as a rum-runner, eventually being caught and jailed by the American authorities for his activities. He never married, and died in Vancouver in 1931 at the age of 58 (see Vancouver *Province* for Sept. 9 and 10, 1931). As he was born in Victoria, his remains were taken there for burial.

[3] See the letter by Edgar Fawcett in the *Colonist* of Feb. 6, 1916. The letter also contains a reference to "Captain William Mitchell, who afterwards took command of the *Beaver.*" Captain Walbran, in his *British Columbia Coast Names* (p. 340) says that Mitchell was born in 1802, came to this coast in 1837, entered the service of the HBC in 1838, had charge at various times of the *Cadboro, Una, Recovery* and *Beaver,* and died in Victoria on Jan. 13, 1876. His obituary in the Victoria *Colonist* for Jan. 14, 1876 confirms this information, with the exception that it gives 1836 as the year Mitchell arrived on the Pacific coast, and also says that he was at one time in command of the *Vancouver.* However, I have not been able to determine exactly when Captain Mitchell commanded the *Beaver.*

The archivist of the Hudson's Bay Company has informed me that, "According to the Minutes of Council, William Mitchell was appointed first mate of the *Beaver* for outfit 1843." His name does not, however, appear on a list of captains of the *Beaver* supplied to me by the archivist, covering the period from 1835 to 1860.

[4] When Rudlin took over command of the *Beaver,* Captain Jagers was given command of the *Grappler.* The *Grappler* was eventually destroyed by fire off Valdes Island in 1883 with some loss of life.

[5] See *Colonist* for October 13 and 20, 1874.

[6] Vancouver *Sun,* September 7, 1968, p. 12.

[7] *Colonist,* Dec. 2, 1867.

[8] His son, Captain F. W. Pamphlet, gave a talk on the *Beaver* to the Vancouver section of the B.C. Historical Society on February 20, 1951. According to the report in the *B.C. Historical Quarterly* (issue for Jan-Apr. 1951, p. 114) "Capt. Pamphlet's father, Captain Tom Pamphlet, first saw Burrard Inlet in 1854 in the S.S. *Otter,* while in search of Cowichan Indians involved in murders the previous year. In 1856 he sailed the inlet in S.S. *Beaver,* and in 1860 became her skipper, carrying mail between Victoria and Nanaimo." I think these statements are open to considerable question. An article by J. W. Whitworth in the Vancouver *Province* for Oct. 19, 1935, however, states: "I recall that when Saunders owned her and Capt. Thomas Pamphlet was master we ran the mail to Nanaimo for about a week." The HBC did not relinquish ownership of the *Beaver* until 1874.

[9] Beaver Rock is in Brown Passage. See the article on the *Beaver* in Captain Walbran's *British Columbia Coast Names.*

[10] Captain Walbran calls him "a generous, good-hearted sailor, who utterly despised anything small or mean," and also tells us that while in charge of the brigantine *Una* in 1852 he had taken a number of gold miners to the Queen Charlotte Islands where they found a considerable amount of ore. In the same year, according to Captain Walbran, the harbor on Moresby Island where the discovery was made was given the name of Mitchell Harbor by Capt. Augustus Kuper of H.M.S. *Thetis*.

[11] Vancouver *Province,* August 13, 1938, p. 7.

[12] "We put in a new boiler, and did away with the old-fashioned "D" valve, and installed an up-to-date Poppett valve, which proved very satisfactory and gave the old boat a new lease of life." (John Fullerton, writing in the *Colonist* for Oct. 18, 1936.)

In a letter to the same newspaper on July 26, 1936, Fullerton had written: "The old boat at this time had a different appearance to what she had when she came around the Horn in 1835. All of her cabins and upper work had been removed and her machinery quite altered. The wood of her hull was, however, as sound as ever, and she would poke her nose up on to mud banks and rocky ledges, while loading or unloading, without worrying about scratching her paint."

[13] Warren was later to become a prominent figure in the sealing industry. During the Klondike gold rush of 1898 he commanded the *Alpha*. Further information on Warren may be found in the Victoria *Colonist* for Sept. 11, 1917, Oct. 2, 1949 and Dec. 31. 1950.

[14] See John Fullerton's article "My Days Aboard the Beaver" in the *BCHQ* for July 1938. His connection with the ship apparently ceased in 1879, for when interviewed by the Vancouver *Daily Province* on August 15, 1936 he declared, "I spent two very pleasant and profitable years on the old vessel and learned everything possible about that kind of engine." This issue of the *Province* gives the date that Fullerton became engineer of the *Beaver* as 1867, but this is clearly a misprint.

[15] Sir James Douglas died on August 2, 1877.

[16] After the *Beaver* was laid up, Captain Jagers joined the steamer *Barbara Boscowitz* as purser, and was active along the northern coast of B.C. during 1885. He later took charge of the steam yacht *Saturna* for Messrs. Pike and Payne, and ran it until the vessel was sold in the spring of 1888. He then joined the Canadian Pacific Navigation Company and worked on the *Princess Louise, R. P. Rithet,* and *Yosemite.*

Soon after his arrival in Victoria, Capt. Jagers married Rosina Helen Winger (born in Victoria in 1864, her parents having arrived there on the Robert Lowe in 1862). The Jagers had three children: two daughters, Hazel and Vivian, and a son Claude. The latter became purser of the stern-wheeler *Transfer,* but died at an early age from typhoid fever, apparently contracted from drinking the water of the Fraser River. One daughter became Mrs. Vivian Mills of Victoria, and the other Mrs. Hazel Brown, now of Hartford, Connecticut. My information on Captain Jagers is derived from correspondence with Mrs. Brown and her daughter, Mrs. John Carlin Haley of North Haven, Connecticut, and from Lewis and Dryden's *Marine History of the Pacific Northwest* (p. 311).

Captain Jagers died of cancer on Sept. 3, 1898, and is buried in Ross Bay Cemetery, the Victoria *Daily Times* according him a long obituary, and the *Colonist* noting his "genial disposition and obliging nature", declaring they had won for him "the esteem and respect of a very large circle of friends".

[17] See *Colonist* for February 5, 1879. The buildings were uninsured. There is a picture of the farm house in the *Colonist* for May 14, 1950.

[18] Gabriola Reef has since been known as Thrasher Reef. See Victoria *Colonist* for Nov. 28, 1937, page four of magazine section.

[19] See the article about Thurlow in the *Beaver* for June 1953. He recalled that the *Beaver* used 40 cords of wood every 24 hours. After the *Beaver* was wrecked in 1888, Thurlow secured some of the metal from it and made it into miniature propellors.

[20] A camel (the word is of Dutch origin) is a machine for lifting ships. A water-tight structure is filled with water and then attached to a sunken ship. The camel is then pumped out, which raises the ship. (See Vancouver *Daily Province* for Oct. 9, 1937, p. 4.)

[21] The ownership of various islands between Vancouver Island and Puget Sound was settled by the arbitration of the Kaiser in 1872. The exact location of the boundary between the Alaskan panhandle and B.C. was not settled until the early years of this century.

[22] Alberta and Saskatchewan were not yet provinces, but the HBC had relinquished its rights in this region to the Dominion of Canada.

[23] The *Otter* had been dismantled in March of this year; its hull was used as a coal lighter until 1890, when it was burned for its copper (Lewis and Dryden, *Marine History of the Pacific Northwest,* p. 46).

[24] For example, Captain Marchant later declared that the crew slept on board for the remainder of the night after the ship grounded. It has also been stated that a most plentiful lack of liquor was discovered not long after the *Beaver* sailed, that it was decided to return to port to remedy this defect, and that the accident was due to Marchant cutting his turn too close. See Early Vancouver, unpublished MS by Major Matthews, Vol. 7, p. 357, and also the article by Captain Marchant in the magazine "Harbour and Shipping" (Vancouver), for March 1919, pp. 129-130. Captain Marchant states in this account that there was a thick fog at the time of the accident, and that the crew went ashore the next morning in a rowboat.

[25] Material in Vancouver City Archives. Evans came to Vancouver from Toronto in 1886 and joined the *Beaver* about a month before the accident.

[26] See, for example, the article by A. E. Goodman in the Vancouver *Daily Province* for July 28, 1929: "I have often clambered on her slippery deck at low tide in search of enough teakwood from her sturdy sides to make walking sticks of to give to my friends in the east, and each time I ventured on board there were others there with axe and saw on the same errand as I was."

There has been some controversy as to whether dynamite was used by the eager souvenir-hunters. McCain (*History of S.S. Beaver,* p. 31) says that it was, and this statement was confirmed by John Williams in a conversation with Major Matthews on July 15, 1948: "I blew up her engines with dynamite and sold the old iron to a junk man" (Early Vancouver, unpublished MS by Major Matthews, Vol. 7, p. 462).

[27] 1891 saw the death of Capt. Pender, R.N., once captain of the *Beaver.*

[28] Captain C. W. Cates of North Vancouver told the B.C. Historical Association in 1947 that his father had offered to salvage the *Beaver* and place it in Stanley Park for $600. (See Vancouver *Sun,* Nov. 19, 1947, p. 17.)

7 Relics and Souvenirs

A broken hulk, forlorn and lost am I;
Above me frown the cliffs in ramparts high;
Beneath, on rocky ledge, I stranded lie.

Around, the hungry waves await their prey;
They surge above my head, and day by day
I crumble as they steal
My life away.

Yet not alone despoiled by wind and wave,
But Man, whom I have served, disdains to save,
And robs me as I sink
Into my grave.

The sea-weed damp and chill binds fast my breast,
Yet deep below, in passionate unrest,
There stirs a hope, a dream
Unknown, unguessed.[1]

But they would not let it be. It was as if they knew that, being part of their past, it was part of themselves. Thus almost from the very day it grounded until now, parts of the old wreck have been removed by souvenir hunters, and any object once connected with the little steamer has been eagerly sought after and preserved.[2] The *Beaver's* story may now be concluded (or rather, brought up to date) by tracing the history of the many relics of it now scattered throughout the Pacific northwest.

The first name to be noted in this connection is perhaps that of Charles McCain, a book-seller whose hobby was the history of the Vancouver area. Not only did he make the most persistent of the early attempts to salvage parts of the old steamer, but he was the first to write a history of it. This little volume, published in Vancouver in 1894, undoubtedly contains some inaccuracies, but is a commendable and interesting tribute to its subject. One striking section of it deals with what is perhaps the only occasion on which the "quest of the *Beaver*" cost a life.

McCain and two friends, Edward Brown and James Menzies, had taken advantage of the unusually low tides in the summer of 1892 to salvage what they could from the wreck, "succeeding in getting almost everything which then remained worth carrying away, even to the walking-beams or oscillating levers."[3] McCain and Brown now resolved to spend the last few hours of 1892 in an attempt to secure the centre portion of the main shaft, described by McCain as "a piece of forging about seven and a half feet in length by six inches in diameter, with an 18-inch crank at each end." They did not expect to be able to take this home with them at the first attempt, but rather to detach it from the wreck so

The Beaver *claims a life*

that it could be towed away later by a larger boat. Accordingly, while most residents of Vancouver were celebrating the end of the old year and the approach of a new one, McCain and Brown, taking a lantern, two axes, a saw, two crowbars, a length of rope, a sledge hammer and a wedge, made their way through the frosty streets, borrowed a four-oared cedar skiff from Linton's boat house at the foot of Carrall Street, and embarked on the waters of Burrard Inlet. All went well until they neared their destination; then the two men suddenly realized that something had gone wrong:

> As our boat shot down the stream, the gently rising round on our right made it appear almost as though we were sliding down a bank of water. Suddenly there was an opening in the trees, in the midst of which stood a small frame building. This, although scarcely discernible, we at once recognized as the storehouse at the south end of the submerged city water pipe lines. As we swept past this clearing, which at once gave us our bearings, and revealed the fact that only a few hundred yards of the channel yet remained, a feeling of uneasiness stole over me as I now fully recognized that we were in the clutch of a most terrific current.[4]

The boat, caught in the tide-rip, which McCain later recalled as "a snowy wall of hissing foam," capsized almost immediately. McCain was able to cling to the upturned skiff, but Brown was swept clear of it. Both men made desperate efforts to close the distance separating Brown and the skiff, but without avail, and McCain's companion, burdened with heavy sea boots, was carried away and drowned. For a time it seemed as if McCain would suffer the same fate, but luckily a wave turned the boat right side up, and he discovered an oar still lodged in its rowlock. By using this as a paddle he was eventually able to get the half-submerged craft to land. Here he found shelter in the home of John Thomas, a rancher on the north shore of English Bay where he spent the night. In the morning, having secured a second oar, he returned as he had come; the first oar, however, which may well have saved his life, he kept on his wall as a permanent memento.

McCain, nevertheless, remained not only interested in the *Beaver* but anxious to draw the attention of others to it. Accordingly, out of metal salvaged from the wreck, he manufactured commemorative medals. The first of these, made about 1891, were 1 11/16 inches in diameter, and carried on one side a reproduction of the ship and the words, "wreck of

McCain's medallions

S.S. Beaver, Lion *(sic)* Gate, Vancouver, B.C.," and, under the illustration, the words "Built 1835." The reverse side of the coin carried the somewhat inaccurate inscription, "This metal is out of the S.S. Beaver, the pioneer steamer on the Pacific, and the first to cross the Atlantic."

A short time later, McCain made a second series of medals; these were similar to the first, but the workmanship was noticeably better, and the coin also carried a picture of Columbus' ship the *Santa Maria,* a reminder that it was now 400 years since that historic voyage. A third series, somewhat smaller in size, was to be made after McCain's death.

For a few years, interest in the *Beaver* seemed to languish. Perhaps this was a reflection of the fact that when a pioneer age yields to an age of relative sophistication and comfort, there is at first a tendency for the latter to feel ashamed of its humble origins. It is usually not till some time later that interest in the early days of a region starts to revive.

We might note, though, that when B.C.'s present stately parliament buildings were opened in 1898, the gavel used for the occasion was one made from the wood of the famous steamer.

Yet it was not till 1900 that one begins to find occasional references to "the old *Beaver*" in the newspapers. In that year, Captain Marchant, then in command of the tug *Superior,* succeeded in sinking it on the first of July. He had been ordered to bring a raft of logs to the Hastings Mills in Burrard Inlet; an accident occurred, and the ship, which was on its maiden voyage, went down. Fortunately, because of the Dominion Day holiday, a number of ships of the Royal Navy were in the vicinity, and all the crew were rescued, the last to be picked up being Sin Chee, the Chinese cook. The *Superior* was easily raised, but the Vancouver *Province* in its issue of July 2 commented acidly that Captain Marchant had now sunk the oldest vessel on the coast at one end of Vancouver harbor and the newest at the other.

Five years went by, a period which saw the death of two former captains of the *Beaver.* On October 28, 1902 Captain Rudlin had given a luncheon on board the *Charmer* to celebrate its three-thousandth trip between Victoria and Vancouver, and in August 1903, commanding the *Princess Victoria,* he had lowered the record from Victoria to Vancouver to three hours and fifty-five minutes. It was a triumph he did not live long to enjoy, however, as the *Colonist* for September 24, 1903, recorded:

A page from the 'Beaver's' skin book, a record of the trading done by the HBC with the various tribes up and down the coast

The arms of the Hudson's Bay Company which formed the stern-piece of the famous vessel

An anchor from the 'Beaver'. The anchor was donated to the Vancouver Maritime Museum by the well-known Cates family of North Vancouver. Its authenticity can be established by the distinctive kink at the lower end of the anchor stem which appears also in the photo on page 31.

A spike used in the construction of the ship

This item at the right appeared in the Vancouver 'Province' in 1925 when an old anchor was recovered. It records the occasion of Capt. Marchant's last public appearance, as he died later the same year. The anchor is now in the Vancouver Maritime Museum, and is little changed, as the photograph below shows.

HISTORIC ANCHOR DRAWN UP FROM NINETY FEET OF SALT WATER

DIVERS at work on the sunken tugboat Radius on Monday found the ancient anchor of the steamer Beaver, first steam craft to ply the Pacific. The mass of iron, when it reached the surface, presented a picture of dissolution. Its wrought iron shank, flukes and cable were deeply cut by rust. Great sea worms, four to eight inches long, were imbedded in the crevices of rust-eaten metal and died there when they saw the sunlight. Small crustaceans were clamped to the iron so tight they seemed to be part of the anchor. Two cast iron balls on the ends of the shank were as sound as the day they were moulded, proving the immunity of cast iron from damage in the sea water.

As the Radius had gone down near the point where the old steamer Beaver was lost, the officials of the Vancouver Dredging & Salvage Co. thought the anchor might have been from the Beaver, and on Tuesday they asked Captain Marchant, last commander of the Beaver, to examine the anchor. The veteran mariner declared the anchor had belonged to the Beaver. It has lain there, in fifteen fathoms, since the old steamer was destroyed at Prospect Point thirty-seven years ago.

Captain Marchant is seen in the picture, standing beside the anchor, while a workman holds erect the heavy mass of metal.

The 'Beaver's' boiler, raised in 1906 by C. C. Pilkey. It is shown here beached in North Vancouver about 1909, and was later acquired by the Washington State Historical Society, which placed it on display near Tacoma.

One of the paddlewheel axles from the 'Beaver'. It was recovered by Fred Rogers who presented it to the Vancouver Maritime Museum.

A bell, now hanging in the Merchants' Exchange, Vancouver, which is believed to come from the dining room of the old ship

Part of the engine, variously called a 'walking beam' or 'oscillating lever', presently displayed at Prospect Point in Stanley Park.

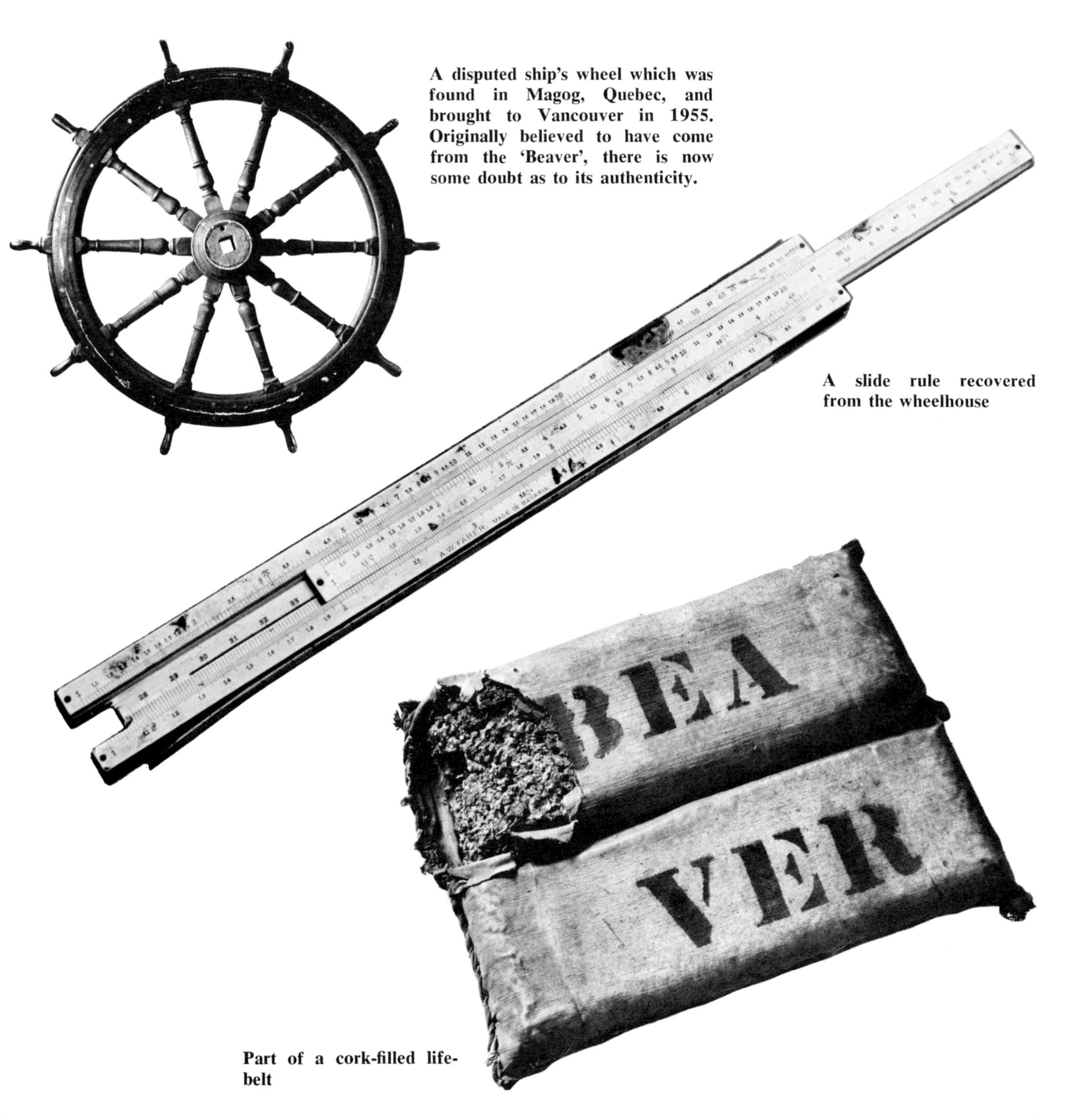

A disputed ship's wheel which was found in Magog, Quebec, and brought to Vancouver in 1955. Originally believed to have come from the 'Beaver', there is now some doubt as to its authenticity.

A slide rule recovered from the wheelhouse

Part of a cork-filled life-belt

Should the Beaver *be raised?*

Captain George Rudlin, the well-known commander of the liner *Princess Victoria,* died suddenly last night in Vancouver. He left the ship, as was his custom, to take a stroll along the Vancouver streets. After reaching the top of a hill, he was puffing and seemed more or less exhausted as a result of the exertion. Feeling weak, he went into the Grand Hotel and asked for a drink of water. While the water was being procured for him, he fell dead. He was 67 years of age.[5]

March 1905 saw the death of Captain Herbert George Lewis (whose wife had predeceased him in 1903), and again the papers paid tribute to the memory of a *Beaver* captain. They noted that he was 77 years of age, had come to Victoria on the *Cowlitz* in 1847, had for a time been stationed at Fort Simpson, and had served on the *Beaver, Otter, Labouchere, Enterprise* and *Princess Louise.* Having left the command of the last-named ship in 1886 to join the marine and fisheries department, at the time of his death he was shipping master for Victoria. Among his varied distinctions, it was noted, were that of being the first man to pilot a steamer through Plumper (Active) Pass, and of never having to make use of spectacles. His wife's brother, claimed the *Colonist,* was the first native son of B.C.[6]

That there was still some interest in the *Beaver* had been shown two years earlier. The *Colonist* for July 9, 1903 had informed its readers that:

> A movement is on foot in Vancouver to petition the provincial government to raise the venerable timbers of the steamer *Beaver,* patch them up and place them on permanent exhibition. When the *Beaver* was stranded on the rocks before she fell to pieces, the City Council at Vancouver was urged time and again to have the ship carried bodily to some safe place on the land, and an attempt was even made by a Victoria man to raise capital to have the boat shipped to the World's Fair. Portions of this steamer, the first to cross the Pacific *(sic),* can still be seen above water at low tide.

The same year, attention was drawn to what was asserted to be the life-boat of the *Beaver.* This had for many years been in the possession of Charles Thulin, proprietor of the Malaspina Hotel at Lund, B.C., and was still in an excellent state of preservation. The Vancouver *Province* noted that it was on exhibition at the headquarters of the Vancouver Tourist Association on Granville Street, and would "soon be housed in Stanley Park." The same paper in a later issue remarked, however, that "the boat

The boiler is salvaged

is an exceedingly heavy and cumbersome affair, and judging by its appearance, it may have been a lucky thing that the navigators of the old *Beaver* never required to launch it in a hurry." Two years later, a letter to a Vancouver paper, the *News-Advertiser,* by a British visitor to the city, suggested that the life-boat, "now reposing on the lake-shore" in Stanley Park, should be preserved in the Carnegie Public Library, where, perhaps suspended above the heads of its patrons, it would serve to remind them of their early days. The writer went on:

> Not only would the boat be less subject to destructive influences, but it would afford an opportunity of appending a brief account of the *Beaver* and its history, unknown or forgotten by many, but a notable feature in the opening days of the Pacific coast.[8]

The fate of this proposal is not clear, but the following year a more ambitious project was successfully carried out by a Vancouver citizen. The *Colonist* of October 2, 1906 recorded the event:

> The boilers of the old steamer *Beaver* were successfully brought to the surface yesterday by Mr. C. C. Pilkey, who has been working on the wreck for some time . . . Mr. Pilkey used scows and tackle capable of lifting 60 tons. He stationed them and passed heavy boom chains through the tubes of the boilers and then brought them up over massive timbers laid across the scows. Three weeks ago a similar attempt failed because a steamer coming past at the time raised a wash which disturbed the scows and slid the timbers out of place. Yesterday morning at low tide he was more successful, and hopes to have the boilers landed high and dry tomorrow morning.

Events clearly moved at a leisurely pace in those days, for the following spring the *Colonist* reported that the boilers, which it described as 22 feet long by 9 inches in height, with a total weight of 30 tons and steam pressure rated at 15 pounds, were lying on the beach near the Heatley Avenue wharf, and that Mr. Pilkey had offered to sell them to the city of Vancouver, "believing that placed in proper position in Stanley Park it would be of great interest to the many visitors to the city."

In the fall of 1908, further progress was reported in recovering relics of the old steamer:

> An attempt is being made to recover the last relics of the famous old steamer *Beaver,* lying on the rocks at Prospect Point, and C. C. Pilkey, who has the exclusive privilege of whatever is left of the steamer, is carrying out the operations. The special inducement for the raising of the remaining portions of the

Beaver lies in the fact that both Seattle and Tacoma are anxious to secure it for the purpose of adding them to their exhibits at the A. Y. P. fair at Seattle next year. Tacoma is willing to take all of the relics and prepare them in an elaborate manner, with electrical and other displays, if given that privilege.

Yesterday morning Mr. Pilkey and Rev. Dr. Osterhout of Vernon, an ardent enthusiast for the preservation of the remnants of the old vessel, went out to the spot and made an attempt to recover the remaining crank-shaft. The other shaft was recovered by parties and melted down. The boiler of the old *Beaver* is now lying on the beach at North Vancouver.[10]

The shaft was evidently raised soon afterward, for the *Colonist* of January 9, 1909 noted that "two years ago Mr. Pilkey lifted the boiler and the shaft was raised two months ago." The same issue noted that he had moved from Vancouver to Vernon, and was still offering the relics for sale. This news item apparently caught the attention of a steamship inspector, J. A. Thomson, for he wrote to the *Colonist* a week later to point out that the recovered boiler was by no means the original one, but one built in 1877 by Joseph Spratt at the Albion Iron Works at Victoria. He also commented:

If we could save the cylinders, entablature, and jet condenser, they are almost the only parts that would be actually of the original structure as from the works of Boulton and Watt. These should not be allowed to leave the province of British Columbia.

No Canadians seemed interested in purchasing Mr. Pilkey's relics, and the boiler was eventually bought by the Washington Historical Society, and placed on display near Tacoma; there, if it was no longer in Canada, it was at least in what had once been part of the "Oregon Territory."[11]

Another portion of the *Beaver* was placed on display a few years later. This was one of its masts, which in 1913 was converted into a flag-pole and erected in a conspicious position (with a somewhat inaccurate inscription)[12] in Stanley Park. There has been some controversy as to the exact age of this relic (though none as to its authenticity), and it seems likely that the mast was one added to the *Beaver* after it was retired from service in the Royal Navy.[13]

Within a year of the erection of this memorial to the *Beaver,* the world was echoing with broadsides from far mightier ships. For more than four long years, the eyes of British Columbians were focussed on the North Sea and the muddy battlefields of France and Flanders, and other interests were largely in abeyance. Even amid the universal carnage, however, there was time to notice the deaths of two former captains of the *Beaver.* On March 16, 1916, Captain Thomas Harraden Pamphlet, who had retired from the sea in 1902, died at the age of 80.[14] The obituary in the Victoria *Times* the next day noted that he had gone to sea as an apprentice in the brig *Eston Nab* in 1849, had been present at the bombardment of Odessa during the Crimean War and later had seen the battle of Balaclava. His various commands — among them the *Ino,* the *Violet,* the *Isabel,* the *Sir James Douglas*, the *Beaver,* the *Alexander* and the *Amelia* — were listed, and he was given credit for helping to choose suitable sites for lumber mills both at Alberni and on Burrard Inlet. It was also noted that having with two partners built the schooner *Bonanza,* he used it to transport stone from Nelson Island to make the Esquimalt drydock.[15]

September 9, 1917 saw the death of Captain James Warren, who had been not only a former owner of the *Beaver,* but a prominent figure in the sealing industry.[16]

A sign that not even the greatest war in history could erase the memory of the *Beaver* came early in 1918. As a result of a campaign by Captain W. H. McNeill's grandson Donald Henry McNeill, then a light-house keeper near Victoria, the Oak Bay Municipal Council applied to the appropriate branch of the federal government to have the body of water generally called Shoal Bay officially gazetted as McNeill Bay, its more correct name. The request was granted, although popular usage continued to favor the first-named appellation.

An uneasy peace returned to the world at last, and civilian pursuits once more took precedence. On May 19, 1920 Vancouver held a giant parade, with numerous interesting entries of an historical nature. Among these were representations of Lord Selkirk, founder of the Red River settlement, a Red River cart, a model of the Spanish ship *Sutil* (in which Captain Galiano had explored the Pacific coast, meeting Captain George Vancouver off Point Grey on June 22, 1792), another of the HBC bastion at Nanaimo, a genuine Indian war canoe, 39 feet long and some 70 or 80 years old, and Indians, soldiers and fur-traders dressed in a variety of apparel from that of the days of Charles the Second to the present. The writer who described the parade for the *Province* noted one significant feature of it:

No float attracted more attention than that of the old steamship *Beaver.* The historic vessel had been rebuilt in miniature by the Vancouver Pioneers' Association and she was a splendid reproduction . . . The float was followed by five decorated automobiles carrying the president and past presidents of the association, together with similar officers of the Ladies Auxiliary.

The post-war period that was in reality but an inter-war period was now in full swing. Pleasure had replaced duty as the goal of life, and few of those merrily disporting themselves on the beaches around Vancouver can have given much thought to the wreck of the old steamer rusting in their midst. A few old-timers, however, had still not forgotten it, as was clear from an article in the Victoria *Colonist* for January 13, 1923: It told how a George Cunningham of Port Essington, B.C. had found a picture of the *Beaver* after a search lasting forty years:

The picture, which appears to be a photograph of a water color, shows the *Beaver* in a mild gale on the West Coast in the year 1865, when the vessel was engaged in survey work for the Imperial Government. Shortly afterwards, in course of a trip to the North, she stopped for a time at Port Essington, and during the usual exchange of compliments and gifts, the picture came ashore and into the possession of an Indian princess.

Mr. Cunningham, the son of a pioneer trader of the North, in his youth heard of the princess' souvenir and eventually decided to secure it for himself. This, however, he found to be no easy matter. The *Beaver* had been regarded with veneration by the Indian tribes, and though the picture often changed individual Indian hands, it was retained tightly by them as a people. At one time, Mr. Cunningham went to the length of employing special agents to locate it, but with no success. It was only a few months ago that his long hunt was crowned with success, and the prized portrait was delivered into his possession.[17]

Half-way through this brief gaudy era, another of the *Beaver's* captains began moving into the last shadows. In the summer of 1924, Captain Marchant, now about 80, poor and in ailing health, was admitted to a retirement home in Vancouver; some of his friends aided him financially,[18] and he occupied his time by writing letters to his sister in Cornwall, with whom, though he had not seen her since 1866, he had always corresponded faithfully.

He did, however, emerge at least twice more into

Captain Marchant's last public appearance before his death

the bustling world. The first occasion was when a cairn was dedicated at Prospect Point to the steamer he had once commanded. A distinguished gathering was present, and Judge Howay, who had been responsible for having the cairn erected, gave a speech outlining the history of the *Beaver*. Mrs. Lefevre's verses were recited, the manager of the local HBC trading post (or department store, as it was by now more usually called) also spoke, while Captain Marchant and John Fullerton had places of honor on the platform. The historian Bruce McKelvie described the *Beaver* as "a vessel that meant more than just a means of transportation — a craft with a purpose and a mission, and one of the greatest factors in the development of the white man's civilization."[19] A plaque was provided; it informed future visitors to the spot that:

> Here on 26th July, 1888, the steamer Beaver was wrecked.
> This historic vessel was built for the Hudson's Bay Company at Blackwall, England, in 1835, sailed for this coast immediately and was the pioneer steamship of the Pacific Ocean.
> The story of the Beaver is the story of the early development of the western coast of Canada.

On August 31, 1925, divers working on the sunken tugboat *Radius* recovered an anchor near the place where the *Beaver* had gone down. The *Province* gave a description of it the next day:

> The mass of iron, when it reached the surface, presented a picture of dissolution. Its wrought iron shank, flukes and cable were deeply cut by rust. Great sea worms, four to eight inches long, were imbedded in the crevices of rust-eaten metal, and died there when they saw the sunlight. Small crustaceans were clamped to the iron so tight they seemed to be part of the anchor. Two cast iron balls on the end of the shank were as sound as the day they were moulded, proving the immunity of cast iron from damage in the sea water.

Was this the anchor of the *Beaver*? There was one man who would know, and it was submitted to his judgment. Captain Marchant emerged from his retirement long enough to identify it as indeed the anchor of the *Beaver*, and to be photographed standing beside it.[20]

This was his last public appearance. His health now failed, and on the first of November he was dead.

1925 also saw the son of a former captain of the *Beaver* in the news. This was Captain Robert Pamphlet, who, striving to benefit by the American prohibition laws, found himself sentenced to a term in prison, which he served on McNeill's Island in Puget Sound, named after a captain of the *Beaver*. In an account which he gave to the press, he outlined the dilemma which resulted in his imprisonment:

> I am a rum-runner, but I have always played the game square. On February 3, 1925 I was sailing off the Columbia River when I ran into a storm. I was carrying a load of liquor for sale to any purchaser who might come along. The storm got worse and it took me all my time to manage my own ship.
>
> About 11:30 in the morning I descried signals of distress from a ship that afterwards turned out to be the *Caoba*, Captain Sandwig in charge. I went to the rescue of this ship and succeeded in getting off the captain and nine men . . .
>
> At 5:30 the United States coast guard cutter, in charge of Captain Wishard, came along and challenged me. The captain sent a lieutenant aboard my ship. He demanded to know what I had aboard, and I told him I had a shipload of liquor. Despite the fact that we were thirty miles out at sea, Captain Wishard threw a line aboard and ordered me to hold fast. I did so, and was towed into Portland . . .
>
> I was between the deep sea and the devil on that memorable day. If I had refused to go to the help of the ship in distress, I would have been hanged by the Canadian law, and if I went to its rescue I was faced by a term of imprisonment.[21]

By the time the Captain emerged from prison in August 1929, the gaudy 1920's were about to leap to their spectacular death in the canyons of Wall Street, and soon the nation was caught in the icy grip of the Great Depression. The winds of history began to blow fiercely, and as if to symbolize this, the flag-pole at Brockton Point made from the mast of the *Beaver* came down in a big storm. The Parks Board, however, announced its intention of having the relic repaired and re-erected.[22]

The same year (1935) had seen a modest celebration at Victoria of the centenary of the first sailing of the *Beaver*. The Provincial Archives displayed a number of relics of the famous ship, including the original carved coat of arms from its stern, the name-board from the pilot-house, its engine room bell, an engine valve, some links from its anchor chain, one of its stout ribs, a reamer once used to clear its cannon, and the master's certificate of Captain Marchant. A meeting of the B.C. Historical Association was addressed by journalist-historian Bruce McKelvie, who gave an able account of

'A nail in Hitler's coffin'

the *Beaver's* history. Among those present were Captain William Cotsworth, a former mate of the vessel, and John Fullerton, who had been its engineer in the late 1870's. A piece of the ship's timber was presented on this occasion to the Provincial Archives by a resident of Sooke.[23]

Fullerton, indeed, enjoyed a brief hour of glory. He gave an account of his experiences on the *Beaver* to the press,[24] and his story, under the title "My Days aboard the *Beaver*" also appeared in the *B.C. Historical Quarterly* in its issue of July 1938. He recalled how he had once been a member of a guard of honor for Queen Victoria at Braemar, and a photograph of him in highland costume appeared in the daily papers.

He did not, however, have much longer to live. He died in the fall of 1939, at the age of 87, and so the living links with the *Beaver* were reduced still further.[25]

By this time the world was once again at war. In the summer of 1940 the outlook seemed dark indeed, and it was perhaps only natural that at this juncture the *Beaver*, or at least a part of it, should be thrown into the breach. A Vancouver pioneer, Robert Townley, donated to the "Air Supremacy Drive" a bolt made of solid copper, one foot long and weighing four pounds, which he had removed from the wreck one Sunday in 1889. He suggested that the bolt should be melted down and made into souvenirs, which could then be sold. The fate of this proposal is not recorded, but it is pleasant to imagine that, in a somewhat metaphorical and roundabout way, this fragment of the *Beaver* became a nail in Hitler's coffin.[26]

Indeed, not even the global catastrophe could prevent the *Beaver* from being recalled from time to time to the attention of the public. In June 1941, James William Sinclair, a former purser of the steamer, died in New Westminster, and in July the Vancouver Archives acquired a valuable if controversial item in the form of the "walking beam" or "oscillating lever" of the famous vessel. This fragment of the *Beaver,* about twelve feet long and weighing well over 500 pounds, and whose function was to connect the piston and the paddle-wheel axle, had been removed from the wreck by J. N. Menzies, who had once been the partner of Charles McCain in the contracting business. The relic had then been moved to a series of locations, and eventually had lain almost forgotten for many years under a garage at 672 Cordova Street. The Vancouver City Archivist, Major Matthews, hearing of this valuable piece of B.C. history, persuaded Mrs. Bertha Menzies, by then widowed, to donate it to the city in 1940.[27] The recovery of the relic, and its transfer to the City Hall was not entirely uneventful, as reported by the Vancouver *News-Herald* of November 27, 1940:

> Mrs. Menzies has sold the premises under which it had lain four decades, and gave the Major permission to remove it. Monday, he tore a hole in the floor and found the relic, but Tuesday when plans for its removal were begun, a Japanese who had purchased the building protested loudly and finally sent for the police. The archivist, however, was able to prove official ownership and the heavy casting was removed to the City Hall.

In July 1941 the relic was mounted in Stanley Park, the event being signalled by a little ceremony attended by Mrs. Walter Winsby, daughter of Henry Saunders, the last owner of the *Beaver;* W. H. Evans, who had been the assistant engineer of the ship when it went aground in 1888, and who vouched for the relic's authenticity; and Bill Nahanee, an Indian who had been a coal-passer on the ship at the age of thirteen.[28]

This native son, a member of the North Vancouver Indian Reserve, had a few details to give of the old *Beaver,* as recorded in a conversation with Major Matthews on Sept. 12, 1941:

> So far as I know, Billy Evans and myself are the only two persons living now who worked on the old *Beaver.* I was only about thirteen or fourteen, and worked on the *Beaver* for one day only; myself and another boy were passing coal. The *Beaver* used to come into Moodyville all the time, and one day she wanted some coal, and we got the job packing the coal from forward, where it was stored in the fire room, back to the engineer. It was loose, and we had a wheelbarrow. She was going north to get a boom of logs, and we two boys went as far as Bowen Island or somewhere, and then the boilers sprang a leak, and she had to come back. Then when we got back to Moodyville, I left her.[29]

For the next few years, as the global war raged to its conclusion in the ruins of Berlin and Hiroshima, to be succeeded by a peace so uneasy as to be termed almost from its beginning the "Cold War", little was heard of "the old *Beaver.*" Nevertheless, the Vancouver *Province* for June 17, 1943, reported from Vernon that

> a rare collection of curios, the property of the late Elvin Dixon, has been bequeathed to the Vernon School Board . . . There is a nail

from H.M.S. *Victory*, Nelson's flagship, and a small piece of polished hardwood, cut from the hull of the wrecked steamship *Beaver*.

Also, during the war the Vancouver City Archives acquired a walking stick made from its wood;[30] in 1945 a polished 18-inch desk ruler which had once been part of the old steamer, and in 1946 eleven sturdy pieces of teak, ten inches square and four feet long, taken long ago from the wreck. This collection was to be augmented in 1959 when a heavy iron bar, six feet long, with a ring at one end for a rope, was donated to the City Archives by a Vancouver resident.

It may be appropriate at this point to say something about various bells which may at one time have been part of the *Beaver's* equipment. One such bell came to the attention of the public in 1938 when it was produced by W. G. Ashthorpe, a long-time employee of the Imperial Oil Company, who had once been in charge of the Company's oil barge in Coal Harbor. In his younger days he had been the friend of James Dunbar and his wife, who had been squatters on the eastern shore of Stanley Park. After the death of the Dunbars, in accordance with their wishes the bell, said to have been taken from the wreck by Mr. Dunbar, was given to Ashthorpe.

The bell, made of bronze, was about six inches wide at the mouth and about six inches high. It had two Maltese crosses, twelve marguerites and four other ornamentations on it in raised moulded bronze. It was evidently intended to be hung by a strap, for which a ring had been provided.

Some doubt, however, has been cast on the authenticity of this relic, as the date on it is 1878. It has been suggested in rebuttal that the bell was originally from a Chinese barge, the *Twenty-first of May*, wrecked off Race Rocks on December 10, 1881. This vessel was bought for salvage by Henry Saunders, later owner of the *Beaver*, and it has been claimed that at some time he transferred the bell to the latter vessel.[31]

The city of Seattle also has a claim to possess a bell from the *Beaver*. The Museum of History and Industry has had on display since 1952 a bell, upheld by two green dolphins. This, however, is not claimed to be the original bell of the famous steamer, but an accurate copy of it.[32] The original, however, is perhaps also in Seattle; it was said to have been purchased by Fred Geibel, editor of the Seattle *Marine Digest*, some years ago, and after being on public display, not merely in that city but in Vancouver, to have been lost from sight.[33]

Doubts and controversies

Another bell, perhaps with the strongest claim to authenticity, has unfortunately been lost. According to Sydney Saunders of Alberni (son of Henry Saunders, former owner of the *Beaver*), it was removed from the *Beaver* while it was undergoing repairs on one occasion in Victoria, so as to save it from possible damage, and taken to the Saunders home, being replaced by a cheap substitute. The original bell was then lent by the senior Saunders to a lawyer friend named Snowdon, who placed it on exhibit in his office window, from where it was stolen and never recovered.

The substituted bell, declared the younger Saunders in a letter to the Vancouver *Province* of February 5, 1938, was the one which was later to find a prominent place in the Vancouver Merchants' Exchange at 355 Burrard Street. This was taken off the wreck and given to J. J. Nickson, then engaged in laying the water pipe across the First Narrows (and who was later in charge of building the Elk Lake waterworks, the first modern system for Victoria). It remained for a long time in the Nickson family, until given to the City of Vancouver and hung in the Merchants' Exchange.

Some details of the history of this bell have been given from time to time by members of the Nickson and Saunders families. In 1933 Thomas Ralph Nickson told the Vancouver City Archivist:

> It was mother who presented the bell of the historic steamer "Beaver" to the gentlemen of the Merchants' Exchange, to be placed in their office in the Marine Building; I think you will find an inscription upon it to that effect. It came into her possession through the fact we boys, her sons, and other boys, used to play around the wreck of the old "Beaver" at Prospect Point. We took the bell home, mother treasured it for many years, and it was finally presented to the Merchants' Exchange.[34]

Mrs. Nickson was still alive at this time, and confirmed this account, adding that she "used it for a call to meals at one time—used to strike it."[35]

In a conversation with Major Matthews, Mrs. Walter Winsby, a daughter of Henry Saunders, in her turn confirmed this account a few years later, as well as those accounts which stated that dynamite had been used in dismantling the wreck:

> Father owned the "Beaver." People had no right to go down and tear her to pieces; they even used dynamite. Father complained to the police, but they said she was so far out of town that they could not watch her at that distance.
>
> The *Beaver's* ship's bell and ship's binnacle were removed from the wreck by Capt. Mar-

> chant, her master when she went ashore at Prospect Point, by order of my father, who owned her, and a bell was removed by the boy, Ralph Nickson, son of J. J. Nickson, Superintendent of Construction, Capilano Water Works, and subsequently given to the Vancouver Merchants' Exchange, as you say, by his mother, Mrs. Nickson. It is not, I know it is not, her ship's bell, but the bell from the dining saloon which was rung at mealtime by the steward.[36]

In 1958 a daughter of J. J. Nickson, Mrs. Martha Baylis, explained in a letter to the Victoria *Colonist* on March 30 why the bell showed some signs of damage:

> My father was given the ship's bell from the *Beaver* and for many years we children used to ring it and play with it. When we moved to Sechelt on father's retirement, mother hung the bell on the verandah to call us all to meals.
>
> My brothers used to do a bit of shooting, and often put up a target for practice. Once they had the bright idea of using the old bell as a target as they would not have to go down to see if they had made a hit. Therefore the bell became very battle-scarred. Many years later my mother thought the old bell should be somewhere in Vancouver, where it would be valued as a part of the history of B.C. So she gave it to the city of Vancouver, and it was hung in the Merchants' Exchange.

Bearing this out, the bell at the Exchange has been pierced by a bullet, probably at close range.

There is another relic reputed to be from the *Beaver*, though there is much doubt as to its authenticity. It is a steering-wheel which through the persistent enthusiasm of a Vancouver businessman was finally recovered and placed on display. The wheel, taken to Magog, Quebec by a wealthy industrialist named Bishop, the President of the Foundation Company of Canada, around 1900, was found there by Bill Wright, sales manager of Gault Brothers, in 1940. It was impossible at that time, due to legal complications regarding an estate, to secure possession of the relic; in 1955, however, it was bought for $250 and brought back to Vancouver, being shown for a time in Victoria before finding a permanent home in the Vancouver Maritime Museum.[37]

Subsequent research, unfortunately, has shown that the wheel does not, in all probability, come from the *Beaver* — at least at the time of its wreck, and with the total lack of evidence that it is an even earlier wheel from the ship, its origin will probably remain shrouded in mystery.

The name of Captain W. H. McNeill was still sometimes recalled to the public's attention in this period. 1950 saw the death of two of his grandsons, Robert and Herbert Jesse,[38] and the following year the death of another grandson, Captain Edward Hamilton McNeill at 79.[39] The last buildings of the old McNeill estate in Victoria were demolished in November 1952.

In 1951 the son of another former captain of the *Beaver* was in the news with an interesting suggestion. Captain F. W. Pamphlet of North Vancouver reminded readers of the *Province* for February 21, 1951 that the old wreck was still below the waters of Burrard Inlet "and could probably be salvaged for posterity." He suggested the use of grappling irons to recover it. He himself, however, had but little time to live, dying on November 11 of the same year. The *Sun* for November 13 recorded that he had gone to sea at the age of nine, was a deckhand at 13, had his master's certificate at 17, had been in command of S.S. *Badger* in 1888, and later the engineer of the Canadian National liner *Prince Rupert.* His survivors were listed as three sons, Clayton, Piercy and Fred, a daughter and a sister.

By 1953 there was perhaps only one living link with the old steamer. Captain Eugene Thurlow who, in 1881 had, at age 22, piloted it across Boundary Bay, was still hale and hearty and living in the state of Washington; he supplied an account of those days to the HBC magazine, the *Beaver,* which appeared in June of that year. He recalled that the steamer had used forty cords of wood every 24 hours, and that while towing booms of logs its speed was a mere three knots.

Captain F. W. Pamphlet in his last years had taken part in a controversy regarding the *Beaver.* The question was: did it ever have "walking beams"? Charles McCain, as we saw, had referred to the ship's "walking beams or oscillating levers"; Captain Pamphlet in a letter to the Vancouver *Province* of February 1, 1941 had maintained that the latter was the correct term.[40] Captain Cates of North Vancouver, an expert on ships of all sorts, was inclined to take the same view, declaring in 1953 that walking-beams were an American invention, and did not appear in photographs of the wreck.[41]

Two letters in the *Province* for October 14, 1953 cast some light on the subject, at least for those conversant with technical details. One, by W. N. Cunliffe, stated that:

The old *Beaver* had what is known as a side lever engine. In this type of engine the cylinders are set on their heads and drive upwards to a beam just like that at Prospect Point.

This beam in its turn is coupled to two or more rods which turn the crank of the side paddle wheels. The suggestion that the *Beaver* carried four beams would support my theory that it was a side lever engine, as it would require four of these arms or beams at least if it had two cylinders.

Walking beam engines are much bigger than side lever engines although the side lever type was considered to be more advanced, and developed more power.

Walking beams seldom had more than one very large cylinder, and turned the paddles by one rod between the very big beam and the crankshaft.

In the other letter in the *Province,* A. W. LePage, a long-time friend of Charles McCain, declared that the *Beaver* had twin engines and was equipped with four side levers or oscillating levers, which were carried below decks. He did not doubt, however, that the relic displayed in Stanley Park was indeed a fragment of the famous vessel.

A much more elaborate explanation of the *Beaver's* inner workings had in fact been made twelve years before the publication of these letters. In a conversation with Major Matthews, recorded on August 4, 1941, William Henry Evans, who had been on the *Beaver* the night it sank, expounded the subject in some detail:

You see, the engines of the old Beaver worked like this: First, she had one boiler, it was astern of the engines, and longways across ship, and coal was further astern, and on both port and starboard of the boiler; coal was everywhere we could get it. Then, towards the bow, were the two upright cylinders, about eighteen inches diameter, I don't know what her piston stroke was, and the cylinders were bolted to the engine bed. On both sides of the cylinder were upright iron posts, or guides, and the piston rod was fastened with a nut on the top end to a cross arm on the ends of which were the slides. So then, when the piston went up and down, the slides slid up and down the guides; is that clear? So far so good.

On the outside of the posts, and fastened to the cross arm, were two connecting rods; one on each side, and outside the posts. So, when the piston went up and down, the guides went up and down, and, outside the posts, the one end of the connecting rod went up and down. The other ends of the connecting rods were fastened to the one end of the walking beam.

Souvenirs

At the top left of the photograph is Charles McCain's 1894 history of the 'Beaver', a hard-cover book. McCain also published a keepsake, shown both folded and unfolded, in which he put two of his small souvenir medallions, with a suggestion that they be made into 'serviceable sleeve links', one of which is shown below. The larger medallion was struck earlier, in 1893.

McCain made three types of souvenir medallion, of which the last two are shown on this page. That at the left shows on the obverse the wreck of the 'Beaver' and on the reverse Columbus' 'Santa Maria'. Thus two historic vessels, each with a unique claim to fame, were linked together.

The medallion at the right is smaller than McCain's previous mintings and is that used in his 'keepsake'. It was much used to decorate other 'Beaver' souvenirs.

A walking stick made of wood from the 'Beaver', and a mug made of its metal. Note the medallions soldered to it.

The gavel, made from the wood of the 'Beaver', which was used to open the present Parliament Buildings, Victoria, in 1898. The gavel also has in its head the ubiquitous McCain medallions. At right is a detail from the silver band around the gavel; the other side of the band carries an engraving of the ship.

An ivory bust of Captain William H. McNeill carved from a walrus tusk by an unknown artist

The cairn erected by the Historic Sites and Monuments Board of Canada at Prospect Point in 1924 to commemorate the 'Beaver'. It overlooks the spot where the ship lies on the floor of Burrard Inlet. The text of the plaque can be found on page 123.

Many imaginative souvenirs of the 'Beaver' took the form of a graphic association of it with other historic ships, and here are a few of them. The charcoal drawing, below, by an unknown artist, was for many years in the possession of the family of Edward A. Brown, who lost his life while attempting to salvage parts of the ship in company with Charles McCain.

The two composite photographs on th opposite page depict the 'Beaver' at the en of its career with Canadian Pacific 'Empress ships which were then opening a new era i transportation as they completed the 'all re route' which circled the world.

Down to the Beaver — *recent salvage attempts*

The walking beam: there were four of them, two on each engine, oscillated in a trunnion in their centre, so that when the piston went up the slides went up, and the connecting rod (one end) went up, and the other end pulled up the walking beam, and the other end went down.

On the other end of the walking beam were two or more rods of the same kind, and these two connecting rods were fastened at the other ends to the cranks on the main shaft which revolved the paddles. There were only two cranks on the main shaft, and two walking beams connected by connecting rods to each crank; the idea of the connecting rods was to keep things in line; otherwise the whole machinery, piston and all, would have been wobbling.

The main shaft was in two pieces, connected between the engines with a clutch; so that one engine could go ahead and the other astern.

The two walking beams on each engine were only about twenty inches apart; they had to be, or you could not have got the connecting rods into the crank.

I have forgotten to tell you about the hatchway to the engine room; it was forward of the engine, as the boiler was astern. You went down the hatchway, and then you ducked your head. If you didn't, the beams above would knock your head off; I mean the wooden supports to the deck.

Get it clear: there was one boiler, two cylinders, two cranks, and four walking beams.[42]

At least this technical dispute had shown that there were still those interested in the old steamer. That others besides old salts remembered it, was shown in 1957 when an accurate model of it (1/6 of an inch to the foot) made by Colonel George Ricard of Cordova Bay was sent by the Victoria Chamber of Commerce as a gesture of good will to similar bodies in Fort Vancouver and Portland.[43]

1960, however, was to see a far more dramatic development, thanks to the persistent interest of a remarkable man, A. C. (Fred) Rogers of Vancouver. A veteran diver, he had already been down to numerous other wrecks along the Pacific coast[44] and he now resolved to locate the remains of the *Beaver* and if possible recover parts of it for the benefit of posterity.

His first objective, to locate the wreck, was quickly achieved. The story may conveniently be told in his own words:[45]

On Sunday, September 12, 1960, the writer and Cliff Donovan, Ed Seaton and Gordon Squarebriggs went to the place I had selected as the grave of the *Beaver*. The location was not the easiest place for diving, as the rocks are swept by powerful tidal currents. To make conditions worse, the water is seldom clear, and on the surface the narrows have a steady traffic of ships and boats both large and small.

To reach our destination, we piled our heavy diving gear on Seaton's twenty-two foot boat, and anchored close to shore. One of the important things we had to bear in mind was to avoid coming to the surface out in the channel in the way of boats, and getting carried away by the tide.

Before we went down, I noted that the tide was almost at low ebb and slacking off, which was ideal. We descended by way of the anchor rope, and found limited visibility about five to seven feet. Diving was like groping through dense fog in a late afternoon. We paired off, and the two teams separated in order to expand the search area. I was with Donovan and Seaton was with Squarebriggs.

The marine landscape was as interesting as a garbage dump, and just as varied. Years of pollution from Vancouver showed in forms of broken glass, rusting tin cans, old fishing lines and sinkers, ropes and rusting cables. There were no waving strands of kelp or seaweed to brighten the gray rocks, no colored species of sea-urchins or sea anemones; only a few silt-covered starfish and small fish darted away at our approach.

We stayed close to the bottom and searched carefully for signs of the ship. At twenty feet down, we found a thick growth of umbrella worms with their purple plumes extended. At the slightest disturbance, they retreat inside their fibre tube where they are safe.

From this point, the bottom fell away steeply into deeper water, and was mostly heavy boulders and stones. At forty feet the water was much colder and considerably clearer. We also found a strong current running, and rather than fight it we drifted leisurely with it. Many things catch your attention while underwater; one of them being the heavy and disturbing pulsations of powerful tugs and ships as they pass overhead. Their sounds travel farther and more distinctly in water, and it is quite unnerving for an inexperienced diver, who feels sure the sound is right on top of his head. No signs of the wreck were seen, as the bed of the narrows changed from rocks to gravel and then to sand.

We returned to shallow water and surfaced. As we looked around, someone shouted "The boat!" It was drifting out to sea on the tide. The anchor line had broken, and our next problem was to find the anchor. Ed remained aboard while Donovan, Gordy and I went below to find it. In the gloomy water we soon became separated. While I was probing around the rocks and some decaying seaweed, I noticed something sticking out of the sea-bottom and reached for it. To my surprise, it was a bronze rod about a foot long and an inch thick, imbedded in a buried timber. After some furious twisting and prying, I managed to work it loose. As I examined my find, my eye caught the sight of more brass rods and copper objects scattered about. I quickly gathered up as many as I could hold, and returned to the beach where Donovan was standing in the water. He had been wondering what I was doing on the bottom. When he saw the heavy relics I was holding, however, he came to help me. "It's part of the *Beaver,*" I said, "and there's lots more there."

For the next hour, we were all under water at various times, and by means of ropes we lifted many heavy brass rudder forks and other interesting pieces or iron machinery. Many other large pieces of iron remained buried under rocks and gravel, and would have required something stronger to lift them than our backs and arms.

When our air was exhausted, we called it a day. We had pulled up everything, except Seaton's lost anchor. It had been an exciting day, and well worth the time and effort; we decided that we would return again and explore the area further.

On Sunday September 19th, Seaton, Donovan and I returned to the site of the wreck. The flood tide was gaining speed every minute, a new problem we had not had to face on the previous occasion. We could feel the full force of the tide as it strained on the anchor line. Swimming was out of the question; the only way to move was by pulling myself around from one hand-hold to the next, as if I was mountain-climbing under water.

When I came briefly to the surface, the others decided to also go below, and we made a successful search, uncovering many interesting relics. We found old brass valves, long bronze rods, almost seven feet in length, and some old pieces of copper steam-pipe. We also uncovered some large pieces of an engine for future salvage.

The spoils of our adventure were taken to my garage for storage and cleaning and photographing. We then decided to donate them to the new Vancouver Maritime Museum, whose curator, Mr. Wylie, gratefully accepted them.

Two years later, Rogers made a more elaborate attack on the wreck. He had in the meantime built a thirty-five foot boat with a welded steel hull, fitted with a winch and boom that would lift at least a ton. Rogers and Seaton, accompanied by Cedric Butler, a friend who had helped in the construction of the boat but was not a professional diver, anchored near the wreck on Sunday afternoon, October 21, 1962.

Everything seemed to be just as we had last seen it. We were blessed with better visibility, however, and raised some of the heavy machinery with ease on the winch. I was anxious to do some more exploring, and while Cedric maintained watch on deck, Seaton and I went wandering about in search of interesting objects. Each of us went his separate way, and I soon came across a large object, covered with weeds, and rising several feet off the bottom. I suddenly recognized it as one of the sidewheel drive-shafts.

This was a most important find, and, coming to the surface, I set about finding Ed. I soon traced him by his air bubbles, and found him worrying a bronze spike and some copper sheathing that was fast to some planking of hardwood, like a terrier pulling on an old coat. We surfaced together, had a rest, and recharged our air-tanks.

When I told him about the drive-shaft, we decided to try to lift it. Unfortunately, it proved too heavy for our equipment, and we resolved to try again another time.

Soon, having appealed for assistance through the newspapers, and having received it from Harry Sumner of the Longshoreman's Union, Lyttle Brothers Towing Company and the L & K Lumber Company, the necessary crew, scows, cranes and tugs had been assembled. On the cold drizzling morning of November 5, 1962, the site of the wreck was reached, and Rogers and Seaton went below. The shaft was quickly found, and in a few minutes was resting on the deck of the scow. Later it was presented to the Vancouver Maritime Museum.

This was not, however, Rogers' last visit to the wreck; a year and a half later, he was back on the floor of Burrard Inlet.

Our last visit to the wreck was on April 12, 1964. Ed decided to stay close to shore, while my curiosity led me down a very steep slope into deep water and a mass of huge boulders that levelled off at about 70 feet. I then returned to a slightly shallower depth, and at about forty feet saw what I thought at first was a sunken tree. It turned out, however, to be an old anchor, not far from the other artifacts which had been found by us on previous occasions. I carefully noted the features of the bottom, so I could find it again, and returned to the boat. I found Ed on deck; he had gathered some short copper spikes and pieces

Fred Rogers' salvage operations

Fred Rogers' first expedition in search of the 'Beaver' in 1960. Mr. Rogers is seen at the bow of the boat.

Relics salvaged from the wreck in 1960

Part of the 'Beaver's' machinery lifted at the wreck site during the 1962 salvage operation

One of the 'Beaver's' anchors which was raised in 1964. The anchor has unfortunately since been lost, perhaps for ever.

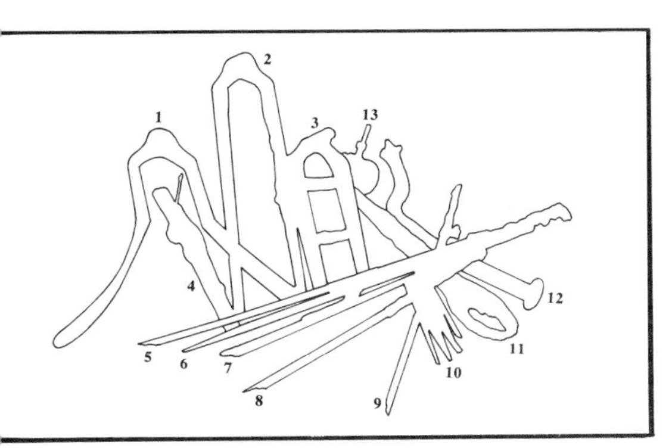

Key to the relics shown on the opposite page. 1 to 4, brass rudder forks; 5 to 10, copper and bronze rods and drift pins to hold the timbers together; 11, iron piece off the engine; 12, copper steam pipe; 13, red copper valve

The Beaver *is reborn*

of wood. I returned below with our cable, and after making it fast, signalled for Ed to hoist it up.

The last act of this drama was in some ways disappointing:

We decided to offer the anchor for sale. This brought forth a protest from unknown people, who informed the marine agent at Victoria of our intentions. I received a notice that the anchor would be confiscated, and that I was to hold it for further instructions.

During the next two months, the old anchor lay resting on the float of Benson's Shipyards in Coal Harbor. It was becoming a nuisance evidently to some people, for they dumped it into the water. We retrieved it a couple of times, but it was once again dropped to the bottom. This time we left it there.

During the month of June, a coast guard vessel called to pick up the anchor. I showed the official where it was, but told him he would need a diver to get it. He promptly sailed away, leaving the anchor to settle down deeper into the black gooey muck.

The fate of the old anchor will probably never be known. During 1968 the area was dredged out for the expansion of the Bayshore Inn, and somewhere in the process the relic of the old *Beaver* probably found a new resting place forever.

So ended, for a time at least, the most determined effort yet made to recover parts of the old *Beaver*. Most of it (its woodwork has long since rotted away and only the metal frame is left) still lies twenty fathoms down, and awaits a larger salvage vessel.

For a time in 1966, however, it might have seemed as if the *Beaver* had been miraculously recovered, and found, like a character in a fairy tale, with all its strength and youth preserved.

It had now been a hundred years since the two colonies of Vancouver Island and British Columbia had been united, and a committee set up by the B.C. government to find suitable means of commemorating the event, decided that a replica of the historic steamer should be built and sent among the various ports of the Pacific northwest, as a reminder of the past which had so firmly and successfully laid the foundations of the present.

The ship, when completed, was in some respects not an absolute duplicate of the original. It was only twenty feet wide, as compared with 33 for the original, and weighed 310 tons as compared with 109. It was converted at Esquimalt drydock under the direction of Lt. William E. Rhodes from an ammunition lighter supplied by the Canadian navy, its steel hull being sheathed in wood, and the deck was raised to make it resemble the original in its middle years. It was put under the command of Lt. Ian Sturgess, R.C.N., assisted by Lt. Robert McIlwaine, R.C.N., and eight seamen. It contained, among other things, an interesting assortment of the trade goods used a century before to barter with the Indians.

Some features of the new *Beaver* were not, however, copied from the old. It was felt that the passage of a hundred years of progress must be saluted as well, and accordingly the ship, powered by two diesel engines generating 300 horse power, was provided with electricity for fans, razors and radios, hot water for showers, a refrigerator, a telephone, and a ship-to-shore radio.

During the summer of 1966[46] the new *Beaver* was on display in many ports along the Pacific coast, affording their residents an imaginative glimpse of the days that were no more. One of those who visited the vessel in 1967, we might note, was William E. McNeill, of Inglewood, California, a hale and hearty 71, and a grandson of one of its earliest commanders.[47]

If one anchor of the *Beaver* was apparently lost from human ken, another now came to the public attention, when it was presented to the Vancouver Maritime Museum by Captain John Cates of North Vancouver and his wife, then mayor of that city.[48] The following document, in the form of a statement sworn before a notary public, will be of interest.

My first knowledge of the S.S. *Beaver's* anchor was in 1911. An old anchor lying on the beach at Eagle Harbor aroused my interest, and on enquiring about it, Mr. Nelson, who owned the property and who subsequently became my father-in-law, gave me the facts of how it happened to be there.

As he told it, he and three other men, all ex-employees of the Hastings Saw Mill, had, in the early days, decided to start up a saw-mill on his Eagle Harbor property. In order to have the machinery for the mill moved from Vancouver, they contacted Capt. Marchant who operated the S.S. *Beaver,* to freight it to Eagle Harbor. In the unloading process, they found the anchor in their way and as Capt. Marchant had another on board, Mr. Nelson jettisoned it, where it lay on the beach for many years.

Shortly after my arrival at Eagle Harbor, my brother-in-law, A. M. Nelson and I purchased a boat. The old anchor was a detriment to our mooring, so we removed the stock and buried the anchor in the sand.

After a move to Vancouver, on occasional visits to Eagle Harbor I would see the stock, but one day, during World War One, I found it gone. It had been sold for scrap metal. A search for it in the Vancouver Yards turned up no trace.

The property at Eagle Harbor was sold after Mr. Nelson's death and later again someone found the anchor and it was taken to Fisherman's Cove, where it was eventually picked up by a Mr. R. McVey who in turn gave it to Capt. Chas. W. Cates.

Through my association with the Nelsons and another relative, Mr. H. Altree, I became well acquainted with Capt. Marchant, by then an old man. Many an evening I spent with him playing cribbage. A fine gentleman who used to say jokingly that he hadn't done a very good job getting the S.S. *Beaver* into Stanley Park.

I declare the above facts to be true,

Earl Ward.[49]

Thus, piece by piece and year by year, parts of the *Beaver* have been recovered, until by 1969 there was a remarkable selection preserved in different parts of the northwest. Indeed, parts of it were as far east as Winnipeg, where the HBC museum has had for many years some of its pulley-blocks.[50]

The Provincial Museum in Victoria, for example, has an interesting collection of relics of the old steamer. These include the griddle iron which Dr. Tolmie had made from the *Beaver's* set of boilers, when they were replaced by new ones in 1843. One may also see the gavel, made of wood from the *Beaver,* which opened the present stately provincial parliament buildings in 1898.

The Maritime Museum in the same city has not only two excellent models of the ship at different stages in its career, but a wheel and two lights said to be from the *Beaver.* Regarding these latter exhibits, a letter by William Inglis of Victoria, their donor, may be of interest:

Regarding your newspaper's reference on June 17 to Mr. Bill Wright's discovery in Quebec of the steering wheel of the S.S. *Beaver,* I would like to inform you the steering wheel and stand and the port and starboard lights were taken off the *Beaver* by a Mr. Carter, who plied these waters along with his father. I was working in his basement and saw the wheel and touched it. He told me these things belonged to the *Beaver.*

I told him that I was installing a steel mast, that I lived at the Mystic Spring, Cadboro Bay, and that I would like to have the wheel at the foot of the mast. "Well," he said, "you can take it. I am too old now to do anything with it."

He said I was the first person to touch it in 50 years.

It is now in the naval museum at the Esquimalt Naval Depot. It is a mahogany wheel and stand, and is badly worn and weatherbeaten.[51]

There has also over the years been an accumulation of vestiges of the *Beaver* of another kind: legends, anecdotes, reminiscences and tall stories. From time to time, various chroniclers of the history of the Pacific northwest have essayed to disentangle from the mass of material the plain unvarnished facts about the famous vessel, although apparently only Charles McCain has ventured to devote a book exclusively to the *Beaver*.

Yet 1894, when his slim red volume appeared, is a long time ago. Since then, much new information has come to light and the resources of scholarship are greater. Now, when the province is preparing to celebrate the hundredth anniversary of its entry into Confederation, it seemed a proper moment to attempt the task anew; to tell once more, as accurately as possible, the story of the little steamer which came across half the world so long ago to lay the foundations of much that today we treasure and enjoy. The result is in the reader's hands.

Footnotes

[1] This poem, by Mrs. L. A. Lefevre, appears in a collection of her other poems in a little book entitled "The Lions' Gate and other Verses," printed in Victoria by the Province Publishing Company in 1895. However, as it is also to be found in Charles McCain's *History of the S.S. Beaver,* published in 1894, it was probably in private circulation before being published. The original title of the poem was "Moritura Te Salutat." (Information supplied by Mrs. M. I. Beveridge of the Vancouver City Archives.)

[2] The first person to realize the historic importance of the *Beaver* was apparently Dr. W. F. Tolmie. In 1843, when new boilers were installed, he had part of the old set made into a griddle iron. This interesting relic is now in the Provincial Museum, Victoria.

[3] Charles McCain, *History of the S.S. Beaver,* Vancouver, 1894, p. 68. These words have since formed part of a complex controversy over whether the *Beaver* ever had any "walking-beams." For some account of this argument, see later sections of this chapter.

[4] McCain, *Op. Cit.,* p. 70.

[5] Captain Rudlin had married Sophia Hill, daughter of John Hill of Warwickshire, in December 1868. Miss Hill and her sister Mrs. Wilcox (who was the widow of the builder of the Royal Hotel in Victoria) operated this hotel after the death of Mr. Wilcox. Mrs. Rudlin died childless about 1912.

Among the ships Rudlin had commanded were the *Princess Louise, R. P. Rithet, Yosemite, Western Slope* and *Islander.* See Lewis & Dryden, *Marine History of the Pacific Northwest,* p. 120, and Victoria *Colonist* for Nov. 3, 1957.

[6] *Colonist,* March 31, 1905, p. 6. It may be noted that the statement in this article that Lewis married Mary Langford in 1852 is incorrect; the correct date is 1870.

It is interesting that the article refers to the "log of the old steamer *Beaver*" as if it was readily accessible; its present whereabouts, except for a small portion dealing with its early years, has for many years been unknown.

Major Matthews, Vancouver City Archivist, recalls seeing it in the HBC store in Vancouver in the closing years of the last century. He describes it as being about 12″ high, 9″ wide, 6″ thick, and bound in leather.

[7] Vancouver *Province,* June 27 and July 6, 1903.

[8] Reprinted in the Victoria *Colonist* for Oct. 19, 1905.

[9] *Colonist,* March 16, 1907. This article incorrectly states that the *Beaver* was launched "under royal auspices."

[10] *Colonist,* Oct. 10, 1908, p. 17.

[11] The boiler is displayed in an open-sided structure adjacent to the Washington State Historical Society's Museum, 315 North Stadium Way, Tacoma.

An article by J. W. Whitworth of Roberts Creek in the Vancouver *Province* for Oct. 19, 1935 states: "It was a low-pressure boiler, allowing eleven pounds of steam, although we usually carried about seven pounds. I recall that when Saunders owned her and Capt. Thomas Pamphlet was master we ran the mail to Nanaimo for about a week. We had to stop the engines to blow the whistle . . . I was on the *Yosemite* and well remember coming into the Narrows the morning the *Beaver* went ashore."

[12] The accompanying plaque said: "This flag-staff was the mast of the S.S. *Beaver,* built by the Hudson's Bay Company at Blackwell-on-Thames, England, 1835. Launched by His Majesty King William IV. The first steamship to come around Cape Horn to Vancouver, and wrecked at Prospect Point, Stanley Park, July 26, 1888. Erected by the Hudson's Bay Company, October 1913."

[13] J. R. Anderson, in a letter to the Victoria *Colonist* of Feb. 24, 1927, says: "In the third stage of her existence, her appearance as a tug was again completely changed by the removal of her two pole-masts, which were replaced by a short pole in her bow for carrying a light. It may be added that part of this pole is that erected at Brockton Point under the impression that it is part of the original mast of the *Beaver.*"

Some writers have asserted that this pole or mast was originally cut on one of the Gulf Islands.

[14] Harraden is the middle name given in the family Bible (photostat in Provincial Archives, Victoria,) though most accounts give the name as Henry.

[15] He was survived by five sons and three daughters, some of these being his wife's children by a former marriage. These were John Cotsford, Capt. T. Cotsford, Mrs. Donald McKay, Capt. T. H. Pamphlet, jr., Fred W. Pamphlet (then chief engineer of the *Petrel*), Robert P. Pamphlet (then chief engineer of the *Lottie*), Catherine Pamphlet and Annie Pamphlet. See Early Vancouver, unpublished MS by Major J. S. Matthews, 5, pp. 198-202.

[16] See his obituary in the Victoria *Colonist* for September 11, 1917. Captain Warren left his widow, one son (George Warren of Seattle) and two daughters, Mrs. George Lassiter of Salt Spring Island and Mrs. E. A. Goddard of Victoria.

[17] The article states that the picture was displayed for a time in the Provincial Museum, later in the office of the Pacific Steamship Company at 911 Government Street, Victoria, and finally taken back to Port Essington.

[18] The administrator of the fund set up for Capt. Marchant was James Hamilton, editor and publisher of *Harbour & Shipping,* who under the name "Captain Kettle" wrote an interesting book, *Western Shores* (Progress Publishing Co., Vancouver, 1932).

[19] See Vancouver *Province* for April 12 and May 8, 1925. The ceremony took place on May 7, 1925.

[20] The picture may be found on page 11 of the *Province* for September 1, 1925.

[21] Undated clipping in Provincial Archives, Victoria.

On another occasion, Captain Pamphlet gave a somewhat different version of his activities: "I am not a rum-runner, nor was I operating as one; I was merely operating a store on the high seas." (Vancouver *Star,* August 30, 1929, p. 5; this article also reported that Capt. Pamphlet "was enthusiastic in his praise of the prison officials.")

Captain Pamphlet died in September 1931 at the age of 58. (Vancouver *Province,* September 9 and 10, 1931.)

[22] See Vancouver *Sun* for September 14, 1935 and the Victoria *Colonist* for the next day. The flag-pole was not re-erected.

The Vancouver *Province* for June 1, 1935 had stated: "Her ship's bell and anchor may be seen in the Vancouver City Museum, and the Hudson's Bay Company Museum in Vancouver has her name-plate on the wall. The best of all her memorials, however, is the flag-staff made from her mainmast, which is erected in Stanley Park and which still flies the flag of the old Company which she served so faithfully."

Regarding the name-plate, Mr. A. P. Horne, a Vancouver old-timer, in a conversation with Major Matthews, Vancouver City Archivist, on April 30, 1936, declared: "Beneath the pilot-house of the old *Beaver* was her name-plate with her name painted on a big board; it is now in the Hudson's Bay Historical Exhibit in their store in Granville Street. A. McCreery and I were walking around Stanley Park one day, and went down to the old *Beaver.* She was falling to pieces; it seemed a shame to leave her name-plate to be destroyed, so we took it off. No one seemed to want it, and I took it home and kept it in my woodshed for some years, afterwards gave it to Sir Charles Piers, Curator, Hudson Bay Company. (Early Vancouver, Volume 4, p. 348. Unpublished MS by Major Matthews, copy in Provincial Archives, Victoria.)

[23] See Victoria *Colonist,* May 9 and 11, 1935. Three links from the *Beaver's* anchor-chain were given to the Vancouver Archives in May of this year by George Adams, Assistant Registrar of Shipping at Vancouver, and these may have been the ones displayed at Victoria.

[24] See *Colonist* for July 26 and Oct. 18, 1936, and Vancouver *Province* for August 15, 1936.

[25] See Victoria *Colonist* for Oct. 20, 1939. Fullerton left a son, John Fullerton of Powell River, and two sisters, Mrs. J. Campbell and Miss Beatrice Fullerton of Victoria.

[26] Vancouver *News-Herald,* July 6, 1940, p. 32. Townley declared at the time, "I had no money and I wanted to help the drive."

[27] See Vancouver *News-Herald,* July 6, 1940. Also Vancouver *Province,* Nov. 27, Dec. 9 and 14, 1940.

[28] See the Vancouver *Province* for July 28, 1941, and the Vancouver *Sun* for July 28 and 30, 1941. Also the article in the *Beaver* for September 1941, p. 48.

[29] See Early Vancouver, unpublished MS by Major J. S. Matthews, copy in Provincial Archives, Vol. VI, pp. 135-136.

[30] There is also one in the Maritime Museum in Victoria.

[31] See Vancouver *Province,* Feb. 26, 1938. Also Early Vancouver, unpublished MS by Major J. S. Matthews, Vol. IV, pp. 71-72.

[32] A letter to the author by Mrs. Sutton Gustison, director

of the Seattle Historical Society, gives the additional information that a plaque attached to the bell's stand suggests that it was a gift from Gerald Frink and Louis Simon to Dick Condon. The museum obtained the bell from a descendant of Mr. Condon.

[33] This bell was on display in 1955 in the window of a Vancouver clothing store on Howe street owned by Murray McCuish, together with the key to the ship's cabin (lent for the occasion by Mr. A. W. LePage), some of its original timbers, and medals made by Charles McCain. Mr. Geibel died in 1957, and the bell was retained by his widow. It has not so far proved possible to locate her, or to determine the present whereabouts of the bell. See Vancouver *Province,* March 2, 1955, p. 3.

[34] Early Vancouver, Volume III, p. 333.

[35] *Ibid.,* p. 335.

[36] Conversation of April 1, 1937. Early Vancouver, Vol. V, p. 317.

[37] See Vancouver *Province,* June 8, 1967, p. 19.
The Maritime Museum of Victoria also has a wheel said to be from the *Beaver,* which it acquired in 1955.

[38] Victoria *Colonist,* May 6 and June 9, 1950.

[39] Victoria *Colonist,* January 30, 1951. Captain McNeill, who at 19 had gone to sea with the sailing fleet, was survived by a daughter, Mrs. George Janak.

[40] In February 1951 in a speech to the B.C. Historical Society he reaffirmed this view, and expressed the belief that the relic on display in Stanley Park was part of the *Beaver's* engines. He declared that only four vessels on the Pacific coast at that time had walking-beams: the *Enterprise, Olympia, Amelia* and *Yosemite.*

[41] Vancouver *Province,* Oct. 6, 1953, p. 21.
On the other side of the controversy, it might be noted that in 1941 Philip T. Timms of Vancouver produced an old newspaper clipping which referred to the *Beaver's* "four great walking-beams" in its lower hold. See Vancouver *Province* for Feb. 1, 1941, p. 8.

[42] Early Vancouver, unpublished MS by Major Matthews, Volume VI, p. 126.
A letter to the author of this book, dated June 18, 1969, from Leonard G. McCann, Assistant Curator of the Maritime Museum in Vancouver, states in part, however: "The item mounted in Stanley Park and labelled the "walking beam" from the *Beaver* is incorrectly designated. It is one of the side levers from her particular style of engine. The *Beaver's* engines were not of a type that incorporated a walking beam."

[43] See Victoria *Times,* March 2, 1957, p. 15.

[44] He had previously brought up the bell of the *Alpha,* wrecked in December 1900 on Yellow Rock near Denman Island. The *Alpha,* built by Cunard in 1875 for the Halifax-West Indies run, came to the west coast in 1898.

[45] Mr. Rogers' account of his various descents to the wreck of the *Beaver* was especially prepared for this book.

[46] This year saw the death on June 12 at Powell River of Captain Stanley Edward McNeill, described as a descendant of Captain W. H. McNeill (*Colonist,* June 17, 1966).

[47] Vancouver *Province,* June 16, 1967.
Another descendant of Capt. W. H. McNeill, Sharon Claudia Robbins, his great-great-great-granddaughter, married Barry William Pearce at St. Mary's Anglican church, Oak Bay in November 1967 (*Colonist,* Nov. 11, 1967).

[48] See Vancouver *Sun* for March 28 and April 2, 1969. There can be little doubt as to the authenticity of this relic. Leonard G. McCann, Assistant Curator of the

Vancouver Maritime Museum notes in a letter to the author that, "The clincher actually is in the anchor itself. In the 1881 photograph, an anchor with a very distinct kink is shown on the port side; our anchor has the self-same kink in the identical location."

[49] The above is copied from a photostat of the original declaration, supplied to the author of this book by the Vancouver Maritime Museum, and dated May 10, 1965. Also enclosed was the receipt, dated March 24, 1949, given to C. H. Cates and Sons in payment for the anchor. The signature is R. A. McVeigh, 262 West 13th street, North Vancouver.

[50] Information supplied to the author in a letter dated May 16, 1969. The blocks were donated to the Winnipeg Museum in 1922 by C. H. French, a HBC employee stationed for many years on the west coast.

[51] Vancouver *Sun,* June 23, 1955.

8 The importance of the 'Beaver'

Yet a few words more. We have come to the end of the story that, beginning in the early years of the nineteenth century, is perhaps not completely concluded in the latter years of the twentieth. One question, however, we have not yet answered, and it is now time to do so. Was the *Beaver* merely an interesting old ship, or was it an integral and vital part of the history of British Columbia and of Canada? Does it deserve all the attention paid to it?

To answer this question, we might first traverse rapidly the period covered by our story. Its basic feature has, of course, been that of change. The Pacific northwest has evolved from a largely uninhabited wilderness to an area pulsing with countless economic activities and with centres of population ranging from thriving communities to large modern cities; fur has given place to gold and this in turn to lumbering as the dominant industry of the area; transportation has become ever swifter and communication almost instantaneous. The Hudson's Bay Company, once the sole source of authority throughout a vast region, has become merely one commercial organization among many, while its chain of trading posts has become a chain of department stores. The rule of appointed officials has given way by gradual degrees to democracy.

Most of these great changes were at least foreshadowed by the time the *Beaver* ceased to navigate these waters, and many chapters of the story were already told. What we should note is that each chapter had the name of the area's first steamer inextricably woven into it. The scattered and isolated outposts of the fur trade along this coast were united by its sturdy engines; the gold miners of 1858 and succeeding years were brought by it nearer to their heart's desire; the great rafts of logs which were later to become the main source of the region's wealth were towed by it at least part of the way toward the markets of the world.

Perhaps most important of all, in deciding the question as to whether what is now British Columbia would be absorbed by the American union or become part of a distinctive culture of its own, the *Beaver,* especially in its early days along this coast, played a highly important and perhaps decisive role. Beyond doubt, by helping the Company it served to withstand and triumph over the economic competition of independent American traders, it did much to affect the final outcome of the contest for the political control of the area to which it had been assigned by "the company of adventurers." It was built as a valuable tool of the fur trade by men who could hardly presume it would become an instrument of Imperial purposes. As a modern scholar has put it:

> The expansion of the British Empire has been largely motivated by the energies of the mercantile class. Far more important to the shaping of British Imperial policy than the secretaries and undersecretaries of state often credited with its formulation were hundreds of men in the commercial community, most of them unknown to history, who created the conditions upon which that policy was based.[1]

Elsewhere in the same work, the same writer repeats this statement in a slightly different form:

> British Columbia became British rather than American or Russian largely because of the work of a small number of fur traders and of the capitalists they represented. Pursuit of profit thus resulted in the expansion of British political authority into northwest America.[2]

Our question as to the importance of the *Beaver* can therefore be answered without hesitation. It was much more than an interesting old ship; it helped to lay the foundations of B.C. and hence of Canada, and as such it deserves the attention of all who today inhabit them.

Now the twentieth century moves toward its close; if there are no great signs that it is to be, as was once confidently proclaimed, "Canada's century," at least it may yet be one in which Canada makes a worthwhile contribution to the common struggle of humanity toward those ideals which seem at once both so close and so elusive. There are larger and more powerful societies than that of Canada, but the more loudly they assert themselves as the harbingers of utopia, the less the evidence supports their claims. The race is not always to the noisy or the brutal.

Thus, more and more, as the overshadowing giants of our time are shown to have feet of clay, the more likely it appears that it may be the smaller countries which will lead the way toward a society of justice. Of such, Canada may yet prove one, and its citizens, conscious of this responsibility, may rightly reflect upon the past out of which their present has emerged. Of this past, "the old *Beaver*" is an important and imperishable part, and those who honor its place in history need fear no embarrassment; their judgment will be confirmed by those who are yet to come.

There is one question, though, on which thoughtful views may differ; what should be done with the frame of the old ship that now rests on the floor of the entrance to Vancouver Harbor? Should it be left alone in the mud and the darkness to sleep its long sleep until the general dissolution? Alternatively, should what remains of it be brought to the surface and displayed where all may see it — or, to put it another way, where it may see what we have been doing in its absence?

Of this we may be sure: Many will remember the historic *Beaver* and inevitably this question of salvaging what is left of it will agitate the imaginative and the enterprising until the wreck is raised — or government decrees that the hulk is not to be recovered or further dismantled until the time when the task may be done effectively and with skill. For after all, the *Beaver* even in the deep, murky, pulsating waters of the Lions Gate is part of our heritage, and should receive the consideration due to so devoted a servant of Canada.

Footnotes

[1] J. S. Galbraith, *The Hudson's Bay Company as an Imperial Factor, 1821-1869,* University of Toronto Press, 1957, p. 3.

[2] *Ibid., Op. Cit.,* p. 174.

Bibliography

Newspapers:

The Victoria *Gazette.*
The Victoria *Colonist.*
The Vancouver *Sun.*
The Vancouver *Province.*
The Vancouver *News-Herald.*
The Vancouver *Star.*

Unpublished Manuscripts in Provincial Archives, Victoria:

ANDERSON, J. R., Notes and comments on early days and events in British Columbia, Washington and Oregon. Victoria, 1925.

COOPER, JAMES, Maritime Matters on the Northwest Coast, Victoria, 1878.

DOUGLAS, JAMES, Diary of a trip to the Northwest Coast, April 22 - October 2, 1840.

DOUGLAS, JAMES, Diary, 1843.

HELMCKEN, J. S., Reminiscences, Victoria, 1892.

MATTHEWS, J. S., Early Vancouver, seven volumes, 1932-1956.

TOD, JOHN, History of New Caledonia and the Northwest Coast, Victoria, 1878.

The Log of the *Beaver,* April 1837 - October 1841.

The Log of the *Convoy,* October 1824 - April 1826.

Periodicals:

The *Beaver,* Hudson's Bay House, Winnipeg.

The *British Columbia Historical Quarterly,* Victoria.

Harbour and Shipping, Vancouver.

Marine Digest, Seattle.

Nautical Research Journal, Whittier, California.

Books:

BANCROFT, H. H., *History of British Columbia, 1792-1887,* San Francisco, 1890.

BANCROFT, H. H., *History of the North West Coast,* 2 volumes, San Francisco, 1884 and 1886.

BOLDUC, J. B., *Notes and Voyages of the Famed Quebec Mission to the Northwest,* Champoeg Press, Portland, Oregon, 1956.

DUNN, JOHN, *History of the Oregon Territory and British North American Fur Trade,* London, 1844.

FINLAYSON, R., *Biography,* Victoria, 1891.

GALBRAITH, J. S., *The Hudson's Bay Company as an Imperial Factor 1821-1869,* U. of Toronto Press, 1957.

HAMILTON, JAMES H., ("Captain Kettle") *Western Shores,* Progress Publishing Company, Vancouver, 1932.

LEWIS AND DRYDEN, *Marine History of the Pacific Northwest,* (ed. E. W. Wright), Antiquarian Press, New York, 1961.

McCAIN, CHARLES, *History of the S.S. Beaver,* Vancouver, 1894.

MACKAY, DOUGLAS, *The Honourable Company,* McClelland and Stewart, Rev. ed., Toronto, 1949.

MERK, FREDERICK (ed.) *Fur Trade and Empire: George Simpson's Journal,* Cambridge, Mass., 1931.

MORESBY, JOHN, *Two Admirals,* London, John Murray, 1909.

MORICE, A. C., *The History of the Northern Interior of British Columbia, formerly New Caledonia,* Toronto, 1904.

ORMSBY, MARGARET, *British Columbia: a History,* Macmillan, 1958.

PARKER, SAMUEL, *Journal of an exploring tour beyond the Rocky Mountains,* 2nd ed., Ithaca, New York, 1840.

RASKY, FRANK, *The Taming of the Canadian West,* McClelland and Stewart, Toronto, 1967.

RICH, E. E., (ed.) *The letters of John McLoughlin,* 3 volumes, 1941, 1943, 1944, Toronto, the Champlain Society.

RICH, E. E., (ed.), *The History of the Hudson's Bay Company,* London, the Hudson's Bay Record Society, 2 vols, 1958 and 1959.

RICH, E. E., (ed.), *London Correspondence Inward from Eden Colvile 1849-1852,* Hudson's Bay Record Society, London, 1956.

SAGE, W. N., *Sir James Douglas and British Columbia,* U. of Toronto Press, 1930.

SCHOLEFIELD, E., and HOWAY, F., *British Columbia from the earliest times to the present,* four volumes, Vancouver, 1914.

SIMPSON, SIR GEORGE, *Narrative of a journey round the world during the years 1841 and 1842,* 2 vols., London, 1847.

TOLMIE, W. F., *Physician and Fur Trader,* Mitchell Press, Vancouver, 1963.

WALBRAN, JOHN T., *British Columbia Coast Names, 1592-1906,* Ottawa, 1909.

Index

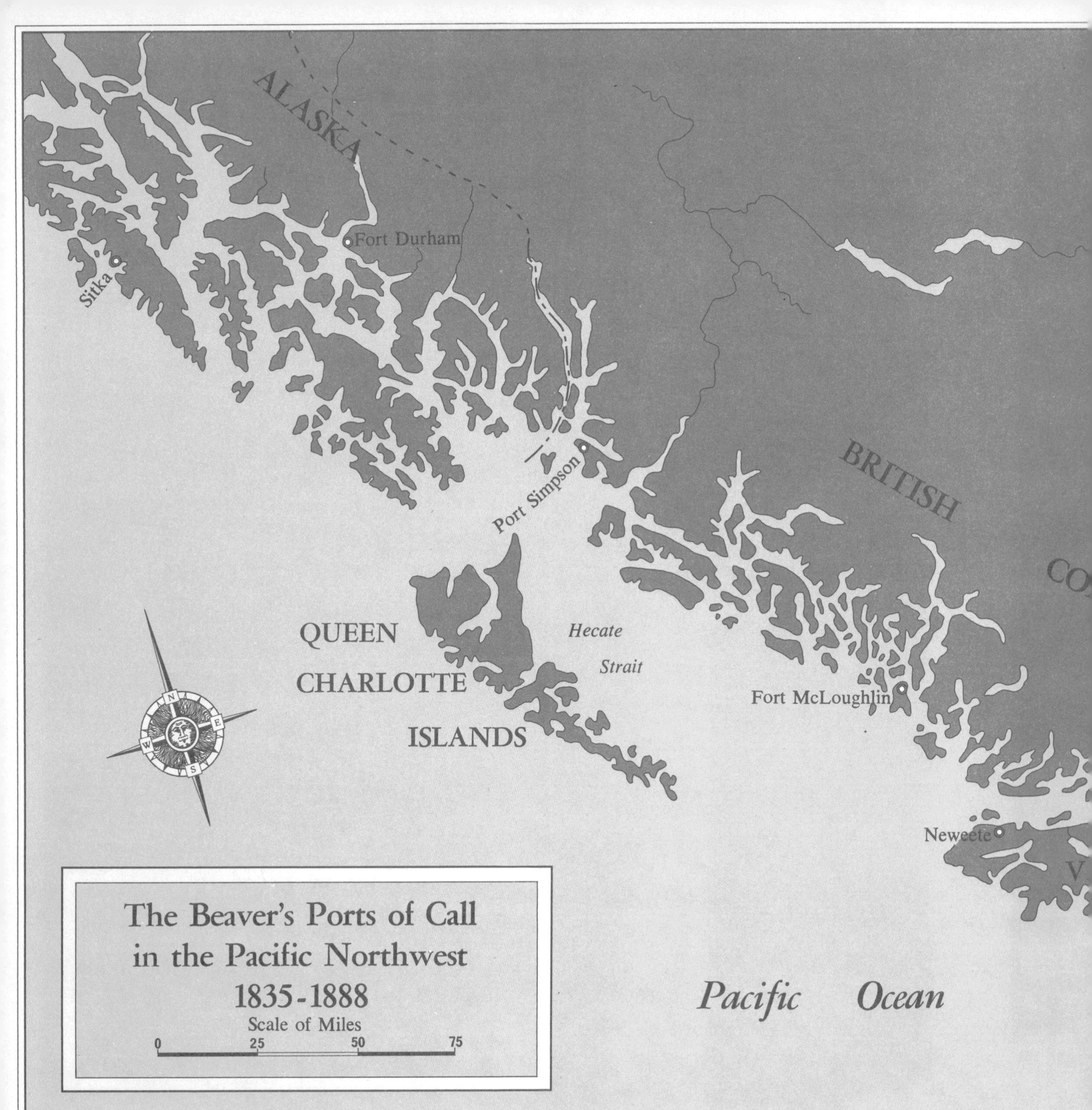
ALASKA
Fort Durham
Sitka
Port Simpson
BRITISH
CO
QUEEN
CHARLOTTE
ISLANDS
Hecate
Strait
Fort McLoughlin
Neweete
N
E
S
W
The Beaver's Ports of Call
in the Pacific Northwest
1835-1888
Scale of Miles
0
25
50
75
Pacific Ocean